To Him,

for whom my spirit yearns.

He, who loves us so much,

and desires that we should have

good health

and good fortune in every thing we do,

so that our everyday affairs may prosper,

just as our soul does.

the *R*eason for writing this book

In 1999, when I decided to join a missionary organization, I set aside my successful career as a realtor and faced the challenge of raising support for my salary. I sat around kitchen table after kitchen table, discussing God's work, the millions of lost souls and my passion for letting people know about the love of God. I visited and talked to over 300 people. I noticed that as long as I talked about the need and the responsibility to fulfill the Great Commission, everyone agreed. But the moment I challenged someone to get involved through financial support, they would share their own financial need.

I felt like the wind had been taken out of my sails. At the same time, something new was being birthed. As God showed me the need for sound financial teaching based on His Word— to help not only the haves but also the have-nots—I felt like He was guiding me into a new field of ministry. Earlier in my life, I personally experienced the power of God's principles when He allowed me to get back on my feet after bankruptcy. These were hard lessons; lessons I believe we learned so that others don't have to. The passion to help others understand God's heart, His will and desires for His children, was ignited. The desire to share what I had learned grew stronger.

This tool has been developed to help you gain personal financial victory through a personal relationship with Christ, by understanding God's principles and by following the leading of the Holy Spirit.

As I have shared my personal experience of how God handles finances, my friends have been fascinated. Upon request, I shared these principles with a small Bible study group that met in our home. As we faithfully studied God's Word and they persisted in the new-found knowledge, they experienced new financial freedom. They finally convinced me to write a book so they could study these principles on their own and share it with others. I combed my journal for every grain of truth God shared with me regarding finances, and how He had led me to gain financial victory. From these, I put together the materials for this book.

Although the names have been changed, the stories in this book are all true. May these life stories and principles speak to your own life and guide you, along with the Holy Spirit, so you don't have to make any of the same mistakes. May God shower His richest blessings upon you as you start this exciting journey.

table of Contents

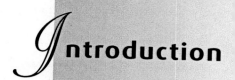

Conventional wisdom teaches that diligence and hard work are the paths to financial freedom. But to lead a successful life financially, and even more importantly, to live victoriously on all levels, does not depend on a formula. We are inundated by the number of books, lectures, seminars and tools available—all trying to show us how to live that successful life.

This is not one of those. Although I am interested in you living a successful, victorious life, I am not offering a formula. That would be easy.

Unfortunately, if we are honest, we all want that easy route. We prefer to follow ten easy steps, buy a lottery ticket, play the stock market, or join another get-rich-quick scheme.

We want a trouble-free life. Free from financial worries—and in order to get there, many of us will do almost anything.

It might surprise you to discover that your relationship with God is in fact the key to a prosperous lifestyle. (We will define all these concepts very carefully in the first week.) God holds a unique plan for your life—a plan to prosper you, and not harm you. All you need to do is yield, understand His principles and live your life by daily seeking His guidance and revelation in His Word.

Success

is neither an inheritance

nor an accident.

It is God's plan for your life.

Look at one kernel of corn.

It has the natural power to multiply.

Abetted by rain, sun and the fertile earth,

there is great potential for future prosperity.

The power is in the seed.

I

GOD AND PROSPERITY

Day 1

GUIDING YOU INTO PROSPERITY

Let the Lord be magnified, which hath pleasure in the prosperity of His servant.

—PSALM 35:27, KJV

It is fascinating to know that God is interested in gold, silver and your personal finances. In Exodus 12:31-38 we read that the Jews left Egypt with wealth and possessions. God made Solomon the richest man on earth. He also made Abraham rich. There are over 2,000 verses in the Bible about money, while 16 of the 38 parables deal with money. Jesus Himself talked about money and prosperous living.

Reflect on the following Scripture verses:

Matthew 7:11

Jesus said, " ... if you then, being evil, know how to give good gifts to your children, how much more will your Father who is in heaven give good things to those who ask Him!"

_____

_____

_____

_____

Matthew 6:30

Now if God so clothes the grass of the field, which today is, and tomorrow is thrown into the oven, will He not much more clothe you, O you of little faith?

_____

_____

_____

_____

3 John 1:2

Beloved, I pray that you may prosper in all things and be in health, just as your soul prospers.

_____

_____

_____

_____

Philippians 4:19

But my God shall supply all your need according to his riches in glory by Christ Jesus.

_____

_____

_____

_____

At a recent financial seminar I heard the following results from an informal survey done with 25-year old persons in North America. It was determined that by the time the group of 100 reached retirement age, it would look like this:

24 out of the 100 will be dead.

54 will be living in poverty

16 will still be working

5 will be financially independent

1 will be wealthy

It was found that 80 percent of 65-year old North Americans don't have $250 in their bank account, while 70 percent of North Americans are one paycheck away from bankruptcy.

The following main obstacles to financial success were identified:

1. Fear
2. Cynicism
3. Laziness
4. Bad habits
5. Arrogance

How you are currently thinking and acting are not likely to bring you to a place of financial independence. In order to understand God's plan for success, you have to make choices that are in line with His direction. You can either speculate and live, or you can get involved in planning your life with God, experiencing *Total Success*. Are you willing to change?

Write a prayer to God, telling Him of your fears and hopes as you set out on this journey to understand His plan for your finances.

_____

_____

_____

_____

_____

_____

_____

_____

Review today's lesson.

1. Prayerfully choose one statement or verse that was most meaningful to you today.

_____

_____

_____

_____

_____

2. Write a prayer of response.

_____

_____

_____

_____

_____

3. What action do you need to take in response to today's lesson?

_____

_____

_____

_____

POWER POINTS
- God is interested in your personal finances.
- One out of every hundred persons will become wealthy.
- God takes pleasure in the prosperity of His servants.
- God's plan for success involves total obedience to His direction.

Day 2

LACK MENTALITY

Christ has redeemed us from the curse of the law, having become a curse for us (for it is written, "Cursed is everyone who hangs on a tree.")

GALATIANS 3:13

God provided a perfect environment for Adam and Eve to live in. They lacked nothing. Today we would probably say they were prosperous. In fact, they did not even know what lack or poverty was. It did not exist in their vocabulary. But when sin entered, a curse was introduced and with that a lack mentality developed. God through a grand (contingency) plan, introduced Redemption through His Son Jesus Christ. Christ came and redeemed us from the curse of the law, as stated in Galatians 3:13. Christ delivered us from the Kingdom of Darkness into the Kingdom of Light.

Scripture teaches us that Christ became poor, so that we might become rich.

Read 2 Corinthians 8:9 (KJV).

For ye know the grace of our Lord Jesus Christ, that, though he was rich, yet for your sakes he became poor, that ye through his poverty might be rich.

Probably your first reaction would be, "Surely she knows that the Apostle Paul is not talking about financial riches!"

What kind of poverty is Paul talking about? In what way did Jesus become poor?

Is it spiritual poverty? I think we will agree that Christ was certainly not spiritually poor. In fact, He was the only person who was spiritually rich and blameless in God's sight, which qualified Him to be the perfect Sacrifice for our redemption. He took our poverty upon Him even as He was hanging on the cross.

But even though God intends to bless us through Christ who paved the way to our inheritance of all spiritual and material blessings, these don't come automatically. Just like salvation isn't automatic, God's blessings need to be appropriated and received. We cannot obtain these through good works or right living, but simply through accepting Christ and His work on the Cross. When Christ delivered us from the curse of the Law, He freed us from that bondage. Just like we pray to receive salvation, we need to bring our poverty before God and receive His blessing through Jesus Christ, and by His grace.

Would you like to pray right now?

_____

_____

_____

The purpose of the Law

Read Galatians 3:19-25 (KJV).

What purpose then does the law serve? It was added because of transgressions, until the Seed should come to whom the promise was made; and it was appointed through angels by the hand of a mediator. Now a mediator does not mediate for one only, but God is one. Is the law then against the promises of God? Certainly not! For if there had been a law given which could have given life, truly righteousness would have been by the law. But the Scripture has confined all under sin, that the promise by faith in Jesus Christ might be given to those who believe. But before faith came, we were kept under guard by the law, kept for the faith which would afterward be revealed. Therefore the law was our tutor to bring us to Christ, that we might be justified by faith. But after faith has come, we are no longer under a tutor.

What was the purpose of the Law in your opinion?

_____

_____

_____

The Law was our tutor and it brought us to Christ. The Law did not have the power to give us liberty. That means our success was Christ's Cross. Obedience and knowledge of the Word of God is the road to success.

God's Word is not complicated. It is very simple. God wants us to each study His Word and be guided by Him through His Word in the steps that we take.

A Metaphor for Salvation

God delivered the Jews out of Egypt and took them to the Promised Land. Not only did the Israelites make this physical journey, it is also a metaphor for our Christian life. God delivered us out of the world (Egypt) and gave us eternal and abundant life (the Promised Land). When Christ delivered us from darkness into the Light, the story of the Jews is paralleled.

Deuteronomy 11:8-9

Therefore you shall keep every commandment which I command you today, that you may be strong, and go in and possess the land which you cross over to possess.

God's first instruction, going into the Promised Land, is to keep His every commandment.

Deuteronomy 11:9

... and that you may prolong your days in the land which the Lord swore to give your fathers, to them and their descendants, "a land flowing with milk and honey."

When Jesus becomes our Lord and Saviour, we come into the Promised Land. Because of our faith in Christ, the blessing of Abraham is ours.

Deuteronomy 11:9-10

For the land which you go to possess is not like the land of Egypt from which you have come, where you sowed your seed and watered it by foot as a vegetable garden.

As we move from the world into the land of our spiritual inheritance, we need to know that it won't be the same. We will have to work and live differently in order to enjoy our milk and honey.

Deuteronomy 11:11-12

But the land which you cross over to possess is a land of hills and valleys, which drinks water from the rain of heaven, a land for which the Lord your God cares; the eyes of the Lord your God are always on it, from the beginning of the year to the very end of the year.

Our idea of a "Promised Land" might be quite different from what the world identifies it as. The spiritual landscape is full of hills and valleys—it is not a trouble-free zone. It drinks water from the rain of heaven—in the Promised Land we are dependent on every Word God speaks to us by His Holy Spirit. Our Lord cares for this land and His eyes are upon it.

Knowing and living by God's Word guides us into living a successful and prosperous life. Our new life in Christ is our Promised Land. Jesus opened the door for us, so that we may live without lack or sickness. The Cross did not only redeem us for the future by giving us eternal life and then leaving us to figure it out by ourselves until we go to heaven. Jesus also took care of our daily troubles. Jesus warned us that trouble will come, but reminded us to be of good cheer, because He has overcome them all. Still, He gives us free will to choose how we want to live our lives, now and through eternity. Living supernaturally is a gift from God. It is free for everyone. But it is our responsibility to take the first step, to move into the realm of living in the supernatural. Total dependency on Christ is the key to this life. Hills and valleys are no longer obstacles, but stepping stones instead.

Review today's lesson.

1. Prayerfully choose one statement or verse that was most meaningful to you today.

_____

_____

_____

_____

_____

_____

2. Write a prayer of response.

_____

_____

_____

_____

_____

_____

_____

_____

_____

3. What action do you need to take in response to today's lesson?

_____

_____

_____

POWER POINTS

- ■ Christ has redeemed you from the curse of the law.
- ■ Our faith in Christ allows us to share in the blessing of Abraham.
- ■ God's blessings need to be appropriated and received.
- ■ He took our poverty upon Him even as He was hanging on the cross.
- ■ Christ became poor, so that we might become rich.
- ■ God's Word will guide you into living a prosperous and successful life.

Journal

GOD

Did you know that God is not only interested in your faith, but also your finances? God cares deeply about your spiritual life, but He is not interested in you as just a spiritual being, but as a whole person. Perhaps that is why Jesus said He came so we might have life and have it more abundantly. (John 10:10) This abundance Jesus spoke of was so much more than financial prosperity. Jesus demonstrated abundance as a way of living and every miracle He did, flowed from this perspective.

God does not separate the spiritual and the financial realms, and neither should we. God is in fact very interested in the state of our bank accounts. It is said that Jesus spoke more about finances than about faith. Perhaps it is because our investments are often a good indicator of where our faith is at. Matthew 6:21 (NIV) says, "For where your treasure is, there your heart will be also.

> So if you have not been trustworthy in handling worldly wealth, who will trust you with true riches?
>
> LUKE 16:11 (NIV)

What do you currently invest most of your money in (eg. stocks, cars, books, an education, a house, missions)?

_____

_____

_____

Would you say the way you allocate your finances accurately reflects your spiritual life?

_____

_____

_____

Reflect on the following two verses and write your own summary.

Song of Solomon 8:7 (NIV)
Many waters cannot quench love; rivers cannot wash it away. If one were to give all the wealth of his house for love, it would be utterly scorned.

_____

_____

Revelation 3:17 (NIV)

You say, "I am rich; I have acquired wealth and do not need a thing." But you do not realize that you are wretched, pitiful, poor, blind and naked.

_____

_____

_____

Money is the lowest form of power in the world. It is temporary. It may provide a temporary solution to pressing problems, but it cannot buy anything lasting or of true value, like love, loyalty, peace or health. You may have all the money in the world and still be poor spiritually, mentally, physically, and socially. It takes the power of God to not only bless you with eternal riches, but to make you rich in every area of life on earth.

Two systems:

There are two choices in front of us: the world's system of prosperity and provision, and God's system of prosperity and provision. According to the *Merriam-Webster's Dictionary*, prosperity indicates a thriving condition, success, and especially economic well-being. As Christians we look to God and His Word for truth. What does the Word say about prosperity?

Reflect on the following Scriptures to gain a greater understanding of God's perspective on prosperity.

According to the Bible, where does prosperity come from?

Isaiah 45:7 (NIV)

I form the light and create darkness, I bring prosperity and create disaster; I, the LORD, do all these things.

Deuteronomy 8:18 (NIV)

But remember the LORD your God, for it is he who gives you the ability to produce wealth, and so confirms his covenant, which he swore to your forefathers, as it is today.

Deuteronomy 28:11 (NIV)

The LORD will grant you abundant prosperity—in the fruit of your womb, the young of your livestock and the crops of your ground—in the land he swore to your forefathers to give you.

1 Samuel 2:7 (NIV)

The LORD sends poverty and wealth; he humbles and he exalts.

Psalm 50:9 (NIV)

I have no need of a bull from your stall or of goats from your pens, for every animal of the forest is mine, and the cattle on a thousand hills. I know every bird in the mountains, and the creatures of the field are mine.

James 1:17 (NIV)

Every good and perfect gift is from above, coming down from the Father of the heavenly lights, who does not change like shifting shadows.

_____

_____

_____

God empowers us to gain wealth. God adds His supernatural blessings to our efforts to accomplish His purpose in our lives.

How do we become prosperous?

Proverbs 21:21 (NIV)

He who pursues righteousness and love finds life, prosperity and honor.

_____

_____

_____

Job 22:21 (NIV)

Submit to God and be at peace with him; in this way prosperity will come to you.

_____

_____

_____

Psalm 128:2 (NIV)

You will eat the fruit of your labor; blessings and prosperity will be yours.

_____

_____

_____

Proverbs 10:4 (NIV)

Lazy hands make a man poor, but diligent hands bring wealth.

_____

_____

_____

Day 3

True Prosperity:

- comes from God

- is God manifesting Himself to us in His Word

- is hearing from God and obeying Him

- is living in peace with Him

- comes through the pursuit of righteousness and love

- is having the heart of a steward

- is not necessarily having lots of money

- is thriving in all areas of life

- is granted by God, but comes as the fruit of labour

- is having God on your side, who holds the ocean in the palm of His Hand

Proverbs 22:4 (NIV)

Humility and the fear of the LORD bring wealth and honor and life.

_____

_____

_____

Where do we find prosperity?

Psalm 112:3 (NIV)

Wealth and riches are in his house, and his righteousness endures forever.

_____

_____

_____

Review today's lesson.

1. Prayerfully choose one statement or verse that was most meaningful to you today.

_____

_____

_____

2. Write a prayer of response.

_____

_____

_____

3. What action do you need to take in response to today's lesson?

_____

_____

Day 3

POWER POINTS

- Jesus came so we might have life and have it abundantly.
- God does not separate the spiritual and the financial realms.
- God is very interested in the state of your bank account.
- Your investments are often a good indicator of where your faith is at.
- Money is the lowest form of power in the world.
- Money is temporary.
- God wants to make you rich in every area of life.

Journal

TRUE PROSPERITY

According to the world's understanding, money and prosperity go hand-in-hand, propagating that one does not exist without the other. But the truth is that wealth and prosperity are completely different concepts and accomplish completely different purposes. The pursuit of money will bring very different results from the pursuit of prosperity.

In your opinion, what is the difference between money and prosperity?

_____

_____

_____

_____

_____

Money is the tool. Prosperity is the experience.

Money as a tool can bring about a prosperous lifestyle, including a large home in an exclusive neighbourhood, designer clothes, exotic cars, beautiful food in expensive restaurants and virtually endless entertainment options. Someone with a conservative income, will not enjoy this same kind of earthly prosperity.

Considering that their health is good and they have solid family relationships and good friends, the person who has a lot of money and the person who has little, are on totally different levels of the earthly prosperity experience. No one would deny that it is fun to have a lot of money. However, very few people pass the test of earthly prosperity to graduate into eternal prosperity.

British historian and essayist Thomas Carlyle said: "Adversity is hard on a man, but for one man who can stand prosperity, there are a hundred that will stand adversity."

Ron Blue agrees and writes, "Prosperity is a test that most people cannot pass."

> But those who desire to be rich fall into temptation and a snare, and into many foolish and harmful lusts which drown men in destruction and perdition. For the love of money is a root of all kinds of evil, for which some have strayed from the faith in their greediness, and pierced themselves through with many sorrows.
>
> 1 TIMOTHY 6:9-10

Even Jesus commented on the test of prosperity. He said, "Again I tell you, it is easier for a camel to go through the eye of a needle than for a rich man to enter the kingdom of God." (Matthew 19:24, NIV)

The Laodicean Church

The Laodicean church was an example of what happens when earthly wealth corrupts spiritual wealth. The Laodicean church was founded in 250 B.C. in a city famous for her beauty and wealth. It was a banking and financial center and produced its own money. In Revelation we read that the Laodicean church had grown accustomed to affluence, and put material wealth ahead of their spiritual needs.

Revelations 3:15-17 (*The Message*) says:

I know you inside and out, and find little to my liking. You're not cold, you're not hot—far better to be either cold or hot! You're stagnant. You make me want to vomit. You brag, 'I'm rich, I've got it made, I need nothing from anyone,' oblivious that in fact you're a pitiful blind beggar, threadbare and homeless.

The Laodiceans allowed wealth to replace faith and failed the test of prosperity.

Why do you think it is so hard to pass the test of prosperity?

_____

_____

_____

_____

Money and the comforts it brings, can easily cause us to take our eyes off the Source.

Money is a temporary tool.

Now read God's instruction to the Laodicean church in Revelation 3:18 (*The Message*)

Here's what I want you to do: Buy your gold from me, gold that's been through the refiner's fire. Then you'll be rich. Buy your clothes from me, clothes designed in Heaven. You've gone around half-naked long enough. And buy medicine for your eyes from me so you can see, really see.

What kind of investments does God recommend?

_____

_____

_____

_____

Who or what is God really talking about here?

_____

_____

_____

_____

Reflect on Psalm 49:5-20 and answer the questions that follow.

Why should I fear when evil days come, when wicked deceivers surround me—those who trust in their wealth and boast of their great riches?

No man can redeem the life of another or give to God a ransom for him—the ransom for a life is costly, no payment is ever enough—that he should live on forever and not see decay.

For all can see that wise men die; the foolish and the senseless alike perish and leave their wealth to others. Their tombs will remain their houses forever, their dwellings for endless generations, though they had named lands after themselves.

But man, despite his riches, does not endure; he is like the beasts that perish.

This is the fate of those who trust in themselves, and of their followers, who approve their sayings. Selah

Like sheep they are destined for the grave, and death will feed on them. The upright will rule over them in the morning; their forms will decay in the grave, far from their princely mansions.

But God will redeem my life from the grave; he will surely take me to himself. Selah

Do not be overawed when a man grows rich, when the splendor of his house increases;

for he will take nothing with him when he dies, his splendor will not descend with him.

Though while he lived he counted himself blessed—and men praise you when you prosper—he will join the generation of his fathers, who will never see the light [of life]. A man who has riches without understanding is like the beasts that perish.

Summarize this Psalm in your own words.

_____

_____

_____

_____

_____

According to the Psalmist, what does money, or earthly riches, accomplish?

_____

_____

_____

Review today's lesson.

1. Prayerfully choose one statement or verse that was most meaningful to you today.

_____

_____

_____

2. Write a prayer of response.

_____

_____

_____

3. What action do you need to take in response to today's lesson?

_____

_____

_____

POWER POINTS
- Money is a tool.
- Prosperity is the experience.
- Whether we are rich or poor, eventually we all die.
- Very few people can pass the test of prosperity.

Journal

_____

_____

_____

_____

_____

_____

_____

_____

_____

_____

_____

_____

_____

_____

_____

_____

_____

_____

_____

_____

_____

_____

_____

_____

_____

_____

_____

_____

_____

_____

_____

_____

_____

_____

_____

THE TRUTH ABOUT ABUNDANT LIVING

> Let your conduct be without covetousness; be content with such things as you have. For He Himself has said, "I will never leave you nor forsake you."
>
> HEBREWS 13:5

Money plays an important part in our life here on earth and determines our abundant living both here now and in eternity. It may not appear like that and we may spiritualize this entire truth just by ignoring the facts. However, when we face the judgment seat of Christ we will have to give an account of our each and every action, including how we handled our money.

In Luke 16 Jesus talked about using your money to prepare a place for eternity. If it is not possible I don't think Jesus would have told His disciples this parable.

A true story about using money for eternity

In 1985 Jack and Lisa, a medical doctor and his wife, met a real estate agent who sold them their first home worth $71,000. They thought the house would be on the market soon.

The agent did not know of any young professionals who would live in such a modest little home but then, she didn't know Jack and Lisa. As Jack read his Bible he found himself compelled to reach for something more and found himself at the start of the generosity process. Luke 6:38 gripped him:"Give, and it will be given to you: good measure, pressed down, shaken together, and running over will be put into your bosom. For with the same measure that you use, it will be measured back to you."

As Jack's medical practice grew, that verse replayed itself over and over again in his mind."Maybe," he confided to Lisa, "the extra money I'm making is not meant for us. Maybe God is increasing my income so we'll have more money to give away."

They faced challenges like tax, investments, children's education—whether to send them to private or public schools—vacation and much more. As a result of their convictions, the couple made a remarkable decision. They set a cap on their lifestyle and resolved not to move the markers, even if their income rose.

If you choose to run life's race with an eternal perspective, what changes can you make now?

_____

_____

_____

_____

_____

_____

_____

Do not spiritualize the truth

God's Word contains His facts and His promises. Our attitude should be like that of a child, receiving from God. We do not give in order to receive, but we definitely acknowledge the facts in the Word of God. If we plant, it will grow.

Pride often keeps us in a religious mode and false humility prevents us from going to our heavenly Father with a child-like attitude. God pursues a relationship with us while we often choose to pursue religion. Satan tries to keep us under the false assumption that we should pursue righteousness by our good works and ignore the practicality of God's revealed Word.

Life was not easy for Jack and Lisa. They had to make many tough choices and had to learn to receive from others. When they decided not to visit their in-laws because they did not want to exceed their spending, their in-laws sent them the ticket. Lisa's parents understood perfectly. Jack saw God's hand at work, and gladly received the blessing.

Jack and Lisa saw God's faithfulness as He met their expenses in ways they could not have imagined. But if they had been unwilling or too proud to receive from others, they would not have been able to enjoy the blessing either.

Do you find it hard or easy to receive from others? Why?

_____

_____

_____

_____

_____

Day 5

Ask God to help you to not only give freely of yourself and your possessions, but also to receive joyfully at His ordained times.

_____

_____

_____

_____

_____

Jack and Lisa put a cap on their spending, by setting boundaries and marking a financial "finish line."

Financial boundaries serve two purposes:

1. They cause you to aim for something and indicate a clear cut-off point.
2. Instead of looking at a formula or a human expert, a God-ordained boundary keeps your eyes fixed on Him as the CEO of your family financial institution.

Since God owns everything, including everything you are managing for Him, every spending decision becomes a spiritual decision. We are always using God's resources. The question is not, "Can I afford this?" but rather, "Would God want me to use His money this way?"

Changing your financial status is a four-step process. You need to:

1. Spend less than you earn.

2. Avoid debt.

3. Build liquidity.

4. Set long-term goals.

Review today's lesson.

1. Prayerfully choose one statement or verse that was most meaningful to you today.

_____

_____

_____

_____

2. Write a prayer of response.

_____

_____

_____

_____

_____

3. What action do you need to take in response to today's lesson?

_____

_____

_____

_____

_____

POWER POINTS

■ We are managers of God's resources.

■ You can use money to prepare an eternal place.

■ God's Word contains His facts and His promises.

■ A financial finish line helps put a cap on your spending.

■ Always ask, "How does God want me to use this money?"

Journal

GOD IS THE SOURCE

When I first started my business I wondered whether God cared about such details as whether I secured a contract or had a good list of clients. I also wondered whether Christians had any advantage over unbelievers or whether salvation only applied to my spiritual life.

Do you think God cares about your business, your work and the financial details of your life? Why?

_____

_____

_____

My God shall supply all your needs according to his riches in glory by Christ Jesus.

PHILIPPIANS 4:19 (NIV)

The farmer's story

There was a farmer who had a big farm where he grew apples, peaches, apricots, cherries, pears, grapes and berries. He took pride in his crops and people drove miles to buy his Elbert peaches.

In a few years, his orchard started to deteriorate and went from bad to worse. He was devastated and related his story to a friend.

"As long as the fruits came each fall, I was satisfied to leave the trees alone," he said. "They bore beautiful fruit." He thought the fruit was his source, because he sold the fruit, made thousands of dollars and fed his family. The fruit became everything to him. It was his business. He depended upon it. He judged everything he did according to how it related to the fruit.

Then one year the crops did not turn out well. The next year there was even less of a yield. While struggling to save his farm, while working in the orchard one day, he realized that the peaches and other fruit were just that—

27

fruit of the tree. The tree was the supplier. He realized that if he took care of the trees, then the fruit would grow. He consulted some experts and slowly but surely started to build up his orchard again.

What state is your orchard in? Are you enjoying good fruit, or are you struggling with meagre crops?

_____

_____

_____

_____

What do you think has caused the state of your harvest?

_____

_____

_____

_____

Who or what do you look to as the source of your fruit?

_____

_____

_____

_____

When we evaluate our needs and try to think of ways to meet those needs, we must remember that the question is never "what is our source," but rather "who is our source." While it may look as if we are dealing with employers, business people, a bad economy or even a good economy—reality is that we are dealing directly with God.

It is very easy to forget, however, especially in our world of multinational corporations, big business, salaries, fluctuating economies, government control and inflation rates that God is our Source; that He is the one who supplies all our needs.

Reflect for a moment on the truth that God is your Source.

_____

_____

_____

According to Philippians 4:19 in what way does God promise to meet our needs?

_____

_____

_____

Take a moment to thank God for being a God of abundant provision.

_____

_____

_____

During the early days of my business, even though I recognized God as my Source, I didn't know how to apply this truth in my daily walk. In my professional life I struggled with how much control to give to God, and how much control to exercise myself. I didn't know when to consult God and when to make my own decisions.

How much do you think is God responsible for providing for your needs (eg. 50%, 75%, 100%)?

_____

_____

_____

What do you think is your responsibility?

_____

_____

God works upon the principle of owner and managers. God is the owner, while we are His managers. God created everything—heaven, earth, the entire natural world, gold, silver, precious stones and finally, Adam and Eve. He formed Adam and Eve in His own likeness and image and then charged them with ruling over the earth. Adam and Eve, along with their descendants, were given the responsibility to manage the earth and its resources.

God, who owns everything, and has all authority, gave us authority to manage the earth on His behalf. Psalm 8:5 even says that He created us merely a little lower than the angels.

God is my Source, while I am the instrument in His Hand by which He meets my needs.

Ask God to reveal to you right now what it means that you are an instrument in His hand by which He meets your needs. Then, listen. Write down anything He might whisper to you today.

_____

_____

_____

Review today's lesson.

1. Prayerfully choose one statement or verse that was most meaningful to you today.

_____

_____

_____

2. Write a prayer of response.

_____

_____

_____

_____

3. What action do you need to take in response to today's lesson?

_____

_____

_____

POWER POINTS

- God is your Source.
- You are a manager of God's resources.
- God has given you the authority to do His work.
- God empowers you to gain wealth.
- You are the instrument in His Hand by which He meets your needs.
- God cares about every detail of your life, including your business.

*J*ournal

Look at the birds of the air, for they neither sow nor reap nor gather into barns; yet your heavenly Father feeds them. Are you not of more value than they?

MATTHEW 6:25-26

JEHOVAH JIREH, YOUR PROVIDER

What kind of Provider is God?

We tend to limit God as our provider of food, clothing and our daily needs. If we give Him the chance, He will run our lives much more creatively than we could ever dream of doing. In my early walk with God, I experienced God's creative and faithful provision. In 1972, when I arrived in the United States, I went to live with a missionary friend in Indiana, while my husband had to live in Louisiana in order to go to university. We had no money, and I started working in a tomato factory. It was very hard work and I earned US$60 per month. Meanwhile, an American evangelist named Brother Campbell went to preach in our hometown in India and lived in our home. When he heard that we needed help financially, he offered me a job in North Carolina. I took the $60 I had earned and went to visit my husband in Louisiana before I would go to North Carolina. We were fasting and praying for a breakthrough. Although my husband was introduced to a famous preacher at that time, this man did not pay attention to our need right then. But since I was in Louisiana, I really wanted to visit the famous preacher. We decided to take a walk to his office, because we did not have the money for a bus or a taxi. Once we started walking, a young man in a car stopped next to us. "I am test-driving my car, do you folks need a ride?" he asked. "I can take you any place you want."

We jumped in the car and he took us where we wanted to go. We both got a job on the spot and even started working that same day. God provides.

Do you remember a time when God met your need in a way only He can?

_____

_____

_____

Take time to review the following Scriptures. Ask God to bring a fresh revelation of these words in your heart.

Matthew 7:11

Jesus said ... if you then, being evil, know how to give good gifts to your children, how much more will your Father who is in heaven give good things to those who ask Him!

_____

_____

_____

_____

_____

Matthew 6: 30

Now if God so clothes the grass of the field, which today is, and tomorrow is thrown into the oven, will He not much more clothe you, O you of little faith?

_____

_____

_____

_____

_____

Isaiah 54: 8-11

For My thoughts are not your thoughts, nor are your ways My ways, says the Lord. For as the heavens are higher than the earth, so are My ways higher than your ways, and My thoughts than your thoughts, ... so shall My word be that goes forth from My mouth, it shall not return to Me void, but it shall accomplish what I please. And it shall prosper in the thing for which I sent it.

_____

_____

_____

_____

3 John 1:2

Beloved, I pray that you may prosper in all things and be in health, just as your soul prospers.

_____

_____

_____

_____

Proverbs 10:22

The blessing of the LORD brings wealth, and he adds no trouble to it.

_____

_____

_____

Philippians 4:19

And my God will meet all your needs according to his glorious riches in Christ Jesus.

_____

_____

_____

Hebrews. 11:6

But without faith it is impossible to please Him, for he who comes to God must believe that He is, and that He is a rewarder of those who diligently seek Him.

_____

_____

_____

Write a summary of what these Scriptures say about God's provision.

_____

_____

_____

_____

_____

_____

_____

_____

God wants to bless us

When God created man in His image and likeness, where did He place him? What was this home and environment like? (See Genesis 2)

_____

_____

What does this say to you about the character of God and His plans for you?

_____

_____

_____

Ask God to reveal to you the life He wants for you.

_____

_____

_____

_____

Psalm 35:27 says God takes pleasure in the prosperity of His servant. From Genesis through Revelations, God shows that He wants to bless and prosper us, if only we will allow Him to do so.

God has a wonderful plan for your life.

Reflect on Jeremiah 29:11 and ask God to open your understanding of this verse in a fresh way. Write down any new insights:

"For I know the plans I have for you," declares the LORD, "plans to prosper you and not to harm you, plans to give you hope and a future."

_____

_____

_____

_____

God's plans for us are always good. He wants to bless and prosper us in every area of our lives.

What does a blessed and prosperous person look like?

Read Psalm 112:1- 6 (TLB) and answer the question.

Praise the Lord! For all who fear God and trust in him are blessed beyond expression. Yes, happy is the man who delights in doing his commands. His children shall be honored everywhere, for good men's sons have a special heritage. He himself shall be wealthy, and his good deeds will never be forgotten. When darkness overtakes him,

light will come bursting in. He is kind and merciful and all goes well for the generous man who conducts his business fairly. Such a man will not be overthrown by evil circumstances. God's constant care of him will make a deep impression on all who see it.

According to Psalm 112:1- 6, what are the characteristics of a blessed and prosperous person?

_____

_____

_____

_____

_____

_____

1. God-fearing; 2. trusts God; 3. delights in doing His commands; 4. kind; 5. merciful; 6. generous; 7. fair

What are the consequences of being a "Psalm 112 person"?

_____

_____

_____

_____

_____

When you seek God first, He will bless you beyond expression. You will be happy and your children will be honoured everywhere. You will be wealthy and your good deeds will be remembered. You will not be overthrown by evil circumstances. The way God takes care of you will make a deep impression on all who see it.

Review today's lesson.

1. Prayerfully choose one statement or verse that was most meaningful to you today.

_____

_____

_____

_____

2. Write a prayer of response.

_____

_____

_____

_____

3. What action do you need to take in response to today's lesson?

_____

_____

_____

_____

If God brings any of these Scriptures to your attention during the day, ask Him what He wants you to do about it. At some point, God may ask you to take note of several of His truths. Develop this into a time of prayer and meditation each day as you ask God what He wants you to do in response to the truths of His provision and your part in it. Ask God to reveal solutions and responses, and write them down. When God speaks, He wants you to pay attention. You may even want to start a spiritual journal for your own reference and benefit.

POWER POINTS

- God takes pleasure in your prosperity.
- God has a wonderful plan for your life.
- Always seek God and His Kingdom first.

REAPING ETERNAL REWARDS

Frank and Shirley's story

Frank and Shirley were clients of financial advisor Ron Blue. They loved the Lord and when they got married, both had good jobs. Their marriage started out well and they soon began raising a family. But when the company Frank worked for went out of business, he was out of a job. He soon found another job, only to lose it six months later when that employer declared bankruptcy. Frank lost job after job and finally decided to start his own company. Unfortunately his company lost money almost from the start. When Frank landed in the hospital for heart surgery, their financial state went from bad to worse and they had to face the credit counselor.

Frank and Shirley's story is not uncommon. Whether it's through the excessive use of credit, a poor business decision, or some totally unforeseen turn of events, like costly medical emergencies or the sudden loss of a job, many of us will, at some point in our lives, find ourselves in a difficult financial position.

Unlike Frank and Shirley, though, our financial problems may not be as obvious or perhaps as severe. At the same time, if you feel that gentle tug at your heart (and you haven't yet done it) it is probably time to sit down and seriously consider your financial position. It took Frank and Shirley more than three years to solve their financial problems. Through the tough times—even when their future looked hopeless—they managed to make giving a priority. When Shirley asked, "Do we really trust God, or don't we?" she knew what Frank's response would be. Despite their difficulties, they had seen God intervene in their lives too many times to doubt His faithfulness.

Frank and Shirley's trust in God turned out to be well-founded. As they undertook their journey towards responsible stewardship, they saw debts forgiven, interest and tax penalties abated, and three refund checks arrive from the IRS! There were several anxious moments, however. Frank had to

> And I say to you, make friends for yourselves by unrighteous mammon, that when you fail, they may receive you into an everlasting home.
>
> LUKE 16:9

have five expensive medical procedures, while Shirley underwent two shoulder surgeries. But all of their medical bills, as well as their original debt, were paid off at the end of three years. Frank and Shirley admit that none of this would have happened if they did not deal with their financial problems on a spiritual level first.

Read the Parable of the Unjust Steward found in Luke 16: 1-13.

He also said to His disciples:"There was a certain rich man who had a steward, and an accusation was brought to him that this man was wasting his goods. So he called him and said to him, `What is this I hear about you? Give an account of your stewardship, for you can no longer be steward. Then the steward said within himself, `What shall I do? For my master is taking the stewardship away from me. I cannot dig; I am ashamed to beg. `I have resolved what to do, that when I am put out of the stewardship, they may receive me into their houses. So he called every one of his masters debtors to him, and said to the first, `How much do you owe my master? And he said,`A hundred measures of oil. So he said to him, `Take your bill, and sit down quickly and write fifty. Then he said to another, `And how much do you owe? So he said, `A hundred measures of wheat. And he said to him, `Take your bill, and write eighty. So the master commended the unjust steward because he had dealt shrewdly. For the sons of this world are more shrewd in their generation than the sons of light. `And I say to you, make friends for yourselves by unrighteous mammon, that when you fail, they may receive you into an everlasting home. `He who is faithful in what is least is faithful also in much; and he who is unjust in what is least is unjust also in much. `Therefore if you have not been faithful in the unrighteous mammon, who will commit to your trust the true riches? And if you have not been faithful in what is another man's, who will give you what is your own? No servant can serve two masters; for either he will hate the one and love the other, or else he will be loyal to the one and despise the other. You cannot serve God and mammon."

The unjust steward was clever enough to use the material things at his disposal to make friends for the future. While the action was unjust, we can learn from the concept.

We are allotted a certain amount of time and material goods in this life. How we use and invest these will determine our future, on earth and in heaven. In this parable, Jesus talked about the shortsightedness of God's people. We often spend our time, money and possessions in view of our present conditions, without considering our lives in the light of eternity.

We will face eternity and we will have to give an account of our time, money and whatever else God had entrusted to our care. We will receive our rewards, our place and our position according to our actions and investments while on earth. While money is a tool for life on earth, it can also be used to invest in our eternal life.

What does eternal prosperity mean to you?

_____

_____

_____

Reflect on Luke 16:8-9 (NIV) and answer the question.

The master commended the dishonest manager because he had acted shrewdly. For the people of this world are more shrewd in dealing with their own kind than are the people of the light. I tell you, use worldly wealth to gain friends for yourselves, so that when it is gone, you will be welcomed into eternal dwellings.

What do you think Jesus meant by this statement?

_____

_____

_____

We can use money as a tool for either a prosperous lifestyle here or in eternity. One has short-term implications; the other long-term. Your perception of life now and for eternity will direct your choices.

According to Jesus' teaching we can prepare for an eternal lifestyle with the money we have on earth. We still have time to change our thoughts and our actions. Jesus offers us this opportunity to live in freedom here on earth, reaping heavenly dividends. Which future are your saving up for?

Reflect on Matthew 6:19-20

Do not lay up for yourselves treasures on earth, where moth and rust destroy and where thieves break in and steal; but lay up for yourselves treasures in heaven, where neither moth nor rust destroys and where thieves do not break in and steal.

Where have you stored up most of your treasures?

_____

_____

_____

_____

How can you store up treasures for yourself in heaven?

_____

_____

_____

_____

Review today's lesson.

1. Prayerfully choose one statement or verse that was most meaningful to you today.

_____

_____

_____

_____

2. Write a prayer of response.

_____

_____

_____

_____

3. What action do you need to take in response to today's lesson?

_____

_____

_____

_____

POWER POINTS

- ■ Consider your life in the light of eternity.
- ■ One day you will have to account for how you have used your time, money and talents.
- ■ You can save up for a heavenly future by storing your treasures in heaven.

$\mathcal{J}$ournal

_____
_____
_____
_____
_____
_____
_____
_____
_____
_____
_____
_____
_____
_____
_____
_____
_____
_____
_____
_____
_____
_____
_____
_____
_____
_____
_____
_____
_____
_____
_____
_____
_____
_____
_____
_____
_____

Beloved, I pray that you may prosper in all things and be in health, just as your soul prospers. For I rejoiced greatly when brethren came and testified of the truth that is in you, just as you walk in the truth. I have no greater joy than to hear that my children walk in truth.

3 JOHN 2-4

PROSPERITY OF BODY, SOUL AND SPIRIT

When John said that we should prosper and be in health he, added the phrase "... even as thy soul prospereth." It is clear in this passage of Scripture that prosperity does not only concern the financial aspects of our lives. Man is a spiritual being and he has a soul, which consists of mind, will and emotion. This spiritual being lives in a "house" we call the body.

Spiritual prosperity

Spiritual prosperity starts when you accept Jesus Christ as your personal Saviour and make Him Lord of your life. It is a journey. You have to stay on the path and abide in Christ in order to grow and prosper spiritually.

John 15: 7
If you abide in Me, and My words abide in you, you will ask what you desire, and it shall be done for you.

What does abiding in Christ mean to you?

_____

_____

_____

_____

_____

_____

_____

Can you remember a specific time when you have abided in Christ? What was the outcome?

_____

_____

_____

_____

What can you do to abide in Christ today and every day?

_____

_____

_____

_____

Soul prosperity

To prosper in the soul is to bring mind, will and emotion under complete control of your regenerated spirit. Christ lives in your heart and He wants to lead and direct your daily life. Simply accumulating enormous amounts of knowledge and information does not make a man mentally prosperous.

Hosea 4:6 says, "My people are destroyed for lack of knowledge. Because you have rejected knowledge, I also will reject you from being priest for Me; because you have forgotten the law of your God, I also will forget your children."

What kind of knowledge does this refer to?

_____

_____

_____

_____

God's Word says that the fear of the Lord is the beginning of wisdom. Wisdom is the principled thing. In the book of Proverbs, Solomon, the wisest man who ever lived, advised us to receive wisdom and also to love wisdom. He told us that the fear of God is the beginning of wisdom. Wisdom is a gift of God to us and in times of need we are to ask for wisdom. But what exactly is wisdom?

Wisdom is the application of knowledge. Knowledge, outside of wisdom, is not totally effective. One word of wisdom from God can change our whole

perspective on life.

Until we invite Jesus into our hearts, we live and operate in the realm of our soul. We deal with our affairs of life according to the direction we receive from our soul. Before the fall of Adam, he operated through his spirit. The spirit gives instruction to the soul, which is processed through mind, will and emotion. The body then responds in the natural world.

We learned that man is a spiritual being and communicates in this physical world through his soul. When Adam sinned, his spirit "died" and his soul took charge of his affairs. God never intended man to operate from the realm of the soul.

When a person receives Christ, his spirit becomes alive again and he receives information from God by which to run his life through his spirit. It is written in the Word of God that our spirit is the candle of the Lord. It is not our soul that is born again, but rather the spirit.

The soul operates in the physical realm by receiving information from the five physical senses. The soul has the capacity to give information and lead you to a level of success, but that success does not have the protection of God. It is open for contest with the corrupted world around us, run by Satan and his wisdom. Therefore, the man who functions from the soul fights and strives to have a real successful life, yet inevitably finds himself in a vicious circle and unable to break free from it. To have an upper hand in life we need Someone more intelligent and resourceful than ourselves.

Do you function through your spirit, or are you ruled by your soul (mind, will and emotions)?

_____
_____
_____
_____
_____
_____

Pray right now and ask God to lead you into a life ruled by the Spirit.

_____
_____
_____
_____
_____
_____

Review today's lesson.

1. Prayerfully choose one statement or verse that was most meaningful to you today.

_____

_____

_____

_____

2. Write a prayer of response.

_____

_____

_____

_____

POWER POINTS

■ Prosperity does not only refer to the financial aspects of your life.

■ Spiritual prosperity starts when you accept Jesus Christ as your personal Saviour.

■ Prosperity of the soul occurs when you bring mind, will and emotion under complete control of your regenerated spirit.

■ God never intended man to operate from the realm of the soul, but through a spirit that has become alive in Christ.

Journal

ESSION II

GOD AND SOVEREIGNTY

49

> But seek first the kingdom of God, and all these things shall be added to you.
>
> LUKE.12:31

A CHANGED LIFESTYLE

Choosing to be a Steward

Read Matthew 25:14-30.

Why do you think did Jesus said in verses 28-29: "Therefore take the talent from him, and give it to him who has ten talents, for to everyone who has, more will be given and he will have abundance; but from him who does not have, even what he has will be taken away."

_____

_____

_____

What is the purpose of this parable?

_____

_____

Where do you stand in relation to this story? What kind of steward have you been?

_____

_____

God is looking for people with the heart of a steward. A steward is simply the CEO of God's business. He puts heart and soul into investing his time, talents, wisdom, and imagination to improve the business of his Master and employer. A steward makes a profit for a company and always has the success of the business at heart.

From the parable we see that the hard-working steward received more responsibility and reward, while the lazy steward received nothing. Even what he had was taken away from him. Both stewards had the same master, but their perception of their master was completely different. They also looked differently at the talents they held in their hands. The one-talented servant reaped according to his own attitude and perception of his master.

God is looking for people who can touch the lives of the lost and the dying. He wants someone who dares to dream big, do His work and fulfill His dreams. To accomplish God's dreams on this earth, we need God's supernatural intervention. God's promise for successful living is conditional. Matthew 6:33 says, "But seek *first* the kingdom of God and His righteousness, and all these things shall be added unto you. (emphasis added)

Luke 6:38 says, "Give, and it shall be given unto you; good measure, pressed down, and shaken together, and running over, shall men give into your bosom. For with the same measure that ye mete withal it shall be measured to you again. (KJV)

Hebrews 11:6 says, "But without faith it is impossible to please Him, for he who comes to God must believe that He is, and that He is a rewarder of those who diligently seek him."

God is more eager to give to us than we care to ask for. He does not hold back blessings from His children.

A good steward chooses to live a God-centered life. That is:

- Confidence in God
- Dependence on God, His ability and His provision
- A life focused on God and His activity
- Self-examination in the sight of God
- Obedience to the best of your ability
- The pursuit of holy and godly living
- Seeking God's perspective in every circumstance
- Seeking first the kingdom of God and His righteousness

Since Christ has redeemed us from the darkness into the light, we are no longer under satan's dominion. We have been given power over this world in His name and by His authority. Although we live in the natural world, as His children, we have the privilege of operating under supernatural law, which produces uncommon results. It's your choice—living under the world's system of prosperity and provision, or living under God's prosperity and provision. Once you have chosen to live under God, the key to success is an obedient heart.

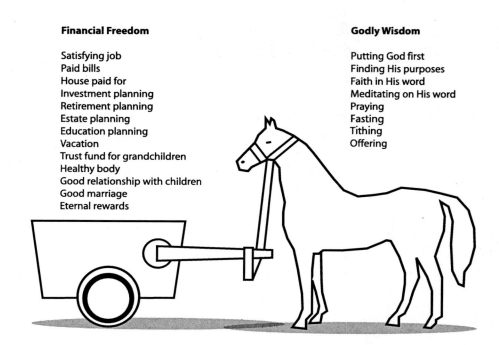

Financial Freedom	Godly Wisdom
Satisfying job	Putting God first
Paid bills	Finding His purposes
House paid for	Faith in His word
Investment planning	Meditating on His word
Retirement planning	Praying
Estate planning	Fasting
Education planning	Tithing
Vacation	Offering
Trust fund for grandchildren	
Healthy body	
Good relationship with children	
Good marriage	
Eternal rewards	

**Putting our cart (our pursuits) before the horse (God's plan)
Seek ye first the Kingdom of God and His righteousness, then
all these things shall be added unto you.**

For additional reading:

1 Corinthians 2:14; Romans 12:2; Proverbs 22:7; Isaiah 58:14

A financial plan that is streamlined for you

Following a plan designed for someone else's life doesn't work. In fact, it usually leaves us frustrated or even hurt. But if you allow God to lead you, He will. Even your relationship with God starts as a seed and takes time to bear fruit. We can never produce fruit without first planting seeds.

Who do usually look to to solve your financial crises?

_____

_____

_____

Who has the best plan for your life, including for your financial life? Why do you say so?

_____

_____

_____

Review today's lesson.

1. Prayerfully choose one statement or verse that was most meaningful to you today.

_____

_____

_____

2. Write a prayer of response.

_____

_____

_____

_____

_____

_____

_____

_____

3. What action do you need to take in response to today's lesson?

_____

_____

_____

_____

_____

POWER POINTS

■ God wants all His children to have the heart of a steward.

■ God's promise for successful living depends upon the attitude of your heart and your obedience.

■ God is more eager to give to you than you may care to ask.

■ As God's child you have the privilege of operating under supernatural law, which produces uncommon results.

■ Living under God's prosperity and provision is a choice.

Journal

KNOWING GOD

Y ou may know about your 'microwave' by reading the instructions but in order to know it through experience, you need to use it. When you want to adopt a puppy, you might do some research about various kinds of dogs and their behavior and come to know about dogs. Once you've chosen a dog, you will get to know it as your pet.

Knowing a human being is more complex than knowing your dog or an electronic apparatus. To know a person intimately depends on whether the person will let himself be known to you. You will know a friend only by how much he allows you to know him.

To know an immortal, all-powerful and invisible God is even more complex than we might think. Since we are mortal and visible, we bring God down to our human level. The word "God" has become so familiar—many use it without thought. We come to know about God through His Word, but we cannot know God unless He lets Himself be known to us.

How well do you know God?

_____
_____
_____

How has God let Himself be known to you?

_____
_____
_____

What do you think you should do to know God? How can you get to know God better?

_____
_____
_____

Before the mountains were brought forth, or ever You had formed the earth and the world, even from everlasting to everlasting, You are God.

PSALM 90:2

Day 2

What does knowing God have to do with your financial matters? Everything. After all, our first and most important business on this earth is to know God. We have been created in His image and we are His representatives on this earth.

Owner and Manager

God created the heavens, the earth and the entire natural world. He created gold, silver and precious stones. He created Adam and Eve in His image and likeness and gave his descendants the responsibility to rule over the earth and manage it. In the "hierarchy" of creation, Psalm 8:5 says that we are created a little lower than God. He created Adam and Eve to manage His Creation. God is the owner; by His grace, we are His managers.

Read Exodus 35:30-35 and 36:1-7.

Why did God make man in His own image and likeness?

_____

_____

_____

Why has God given each of us unique gifts and talents?

_____

_____

_____

God is the Author and Creator of our individual talents; we are the managers of those talents. God gave us talents as tools for creating our prosperity. It is our responsibility to discover our talents and then use them for God's glory.

Ask God today for a revelation of your unique purpose in this world. Who has He created you to be? Which talents has He given you? And for what purpose?

_____

_____

_____

Meditate on the following Scriptures:

Ecclesiastes 5: 18-19

Here is what I have seen: It is good and fitting for one to eat and drink, and to enjoy the good of all his labor in which he toils under the sun all the days of his life which God gives him; for it is his heritage. As for every man to whom God has given riches and wealth, and given him power to eat of it, to receive his heritage and rejoice in his labor this is the gift of God.

_____

_____

_____

_____

Ecclesiastes 6:1-2

There is an evil which I have seen under the sun, and it is common among men: A man to whom God has given riches and wealth and honor, so that he lacks nothing for himself of all he desires; yet God does not give him power to eat of it, but a foreigner consumes it. This is vanity, and it is an evil affliction.

_____

_____

_____

Myths concerning the love of God

John wrote in 1 John 4:8 that God is love and says that love is the focal point of God's moral attributes. It is critically important to understand the goodness of God's love. We usually measure God's love according to our present physical and material circumstances. God sees us in our present choices, but He also sees the end results. His love takes action, with the end result in mind, and He does not compromise His character.

We view God's love through human eyes and many judge God in their hearts. By viewing God's love through the human heart we create a distance between Him and us. Fear often prevents us from consulting Him, from praying or from reading His Word.

In other religions of the world, the relationship between deities and their worshipers is usually marked by fear. It is often expressed in the religious practice of the worshipers as they attempt to prevent the wrath of their deities. They often express the revengeful attributes of their deities. These heretic attitudes have filtered into the body of Christ, reducing God's love to the standard of human love.

In the midst of financial hardship, how do you see God's love?

_____

_____

_____

_____

When you see someone who is wealthy, what do you think about God's love?

_____

_____

_____

The apostle John wrote, "God is love. There is no fear in love ... But perfect love drives out fear. We love because he first loved us." (1 John 4:16, 18-19)

God is all love, all mercy, all grace, all truth, all just and all pure. He deals with us without compromising any of His attributes. While it is beyond our understanding, it is a privilege to be loved by the Almighty God of the Universe who knows everything about us, and still loves us.

Our financial well-being is closely connected with knowing this God of Love.

Reflect on the following Scripture verse:

Psalm 1:1-3 (NKJ)

Blessed is the man who walks not in the counsel of the ungodly, nor stands in the path of sinners, nor sits in the seat of the scornful; But his delight is in the law of the LORD, and in His law he meditates day and night. He shall be like a tree planted by the rivers of water, that brings forth its fruit in its season, whose leaf also shall not wither; and whatever he does shall prosper.

_____

_____

_____

God is faithful to Himself, His Word and His people. He cannot change, because He is perfect. He cannot become better or worse. God is Spirit in the purest sense of the word, which means His actions don't have the limitations of a human being. He is not limited by the properties or characteristics that belong to matter.

God is invisible, He is alive and He is involved with His creation. He is a

Person. He is also eternal. It is difficult to grasp the idea of infinite timelessness with our finite minds, but the Bible tells us that God alone is without beginning. He has always existed and will never end. Deuteronomy 32:40 says, "For I raise My hand to heaven, and say, 'As I live forever.'"

Review today's lesson.

1. Prayerfully choose one statement or verse that was most meaningful to you today.

_____

_____

_____

2. Write a prayer of response.

_____

_____

_____

3. What action do you need to take in response to today's lesson?

_____

_____

_____

POWER POINTS

- ■ I will pursue to know God intimately by obeying Him.
- ■ As I come to know God through experience, trust is established.
- ■ God's love for me is perfect.
- ■ I will not measure God's love through my own understanding.
- ■ God is sovereign, loving, just, holy and powerful.
- ■ His Word stands on its own.

CREATOR OF THE FINANCIAL SYSTEM

As we come to know God through experience, we can shine for Him in this dark world. Without God working in us, we are unable to accomplish His purposes. When God gives us His Word on something, He makes sure that it happens.

Isaiah 46: 9-11

Remember the former things of old, for I am God, and there is no other; I am God, and there is none like Me, declaring the end from the beginning, and from ancient times things that are not yet done, saying, 'My counsel shall stand, and I will do all My pleasure. Indeed I have spoken it; I will also bring it to pass. I have purposed it; I will also do it.

No science, mathematical calculation, nation or individual will ever be able to change the purposes of God. It is simply smart to know the Master and join in His plan to lead an exciting life and experience great things.

Knowing about God and knowing God are two very different things. When we know about God, He might be someone we have heard about, someone vaguely familiar, or even an acquaintance we might call up or bump into once in a while.

When we know God, we enter into an intimate relationship with Him, as if with a best friend. He lets us in on His plans and purposes. He lets us in on what He's doing. Knowing God allows us to share God's perspective and He opens our mind to His way of doing things, eg. the very specific laws He set in place by which He governs the universe.

Read Genesis 1.

In the beginning, God created the heavens and the earth. Then God said, "Let there be light"; and there was light. Then God said, "Let there be a firmament in the midst of the waters, and let it divide the waters from the waters." Then God said, "Let the waters under the heavens be gathered together into one place, and let the dry land

> I have no need for a bull from your stall or of goats from your pens, for every animal of the forest is mine, and the cattle on a thousand hills ... If I were hungry I would not tell you, for the world is mine, and all that is in it.
>
> PSALM 50:10,12 (NIV)

Day 3

appear"; and it was so. Then God said, "Let the earth bring forth grass, the herb that yields seed, and the fruit tree that yields fruit according to its kind, whose seed is in itself, on the earth"; and it was so. Then God said, "Let there be lights in the firmament of the heavens to divide the day from the night; and let them be for signs and seasons, and for days and years"; Then God said, "Let the waters abound with an abundance of living creatures, and let birds fly above the earth across the face of the firmament of the heavens." Then God said, "Let the earth bring forth the living creature according to its kind: cattle and creeping thing and beast of the earth, each according to its kind"; and it was so. Then God said, "Let Us make man in Our image, according to Our likeness; let them have dominion over the fish of the sea, over the birds of the air, and over the cattle, over all the earth and over every creeping thing that creeps on the earth."

What is most significant to you about these verses?

_____

_____

_____

What tool did God use to create our awesome universe?

_____

_____

_____

Yes, the operative words here are "God said." God used words to create the universe and everything in it. In the same way we can use His Word to establish the foundation of what we build on this earth.

Read the following verses and identify two principles God established in the beginning.

Genesis. 1:28

Then God blessed them, and God said to them, Be fruitful and multiply; fill the earth and subdue it; have dominion over the fish of the sea, over the birds of the air, and over every living thing that moves on the earth.

Genesis.8:22

While the earth remains, seed time and harvest, cold and heat, winter and summer, and day and night shall not cease.

Genesis.9:1

So God blessed Noah and his sons, and said to them: Be fruitful and multiply, and fill the earth.

The two principles are:

1. _____

_____

2. _____

_____

God governs His universe by the Word of His mouth. He established the laws of multiplication through seedtime and harvest. These principles are always at work, whether we are aware of them, or not. The good news is that God invites us to join Him in His work. Although our part is very small, it is nevertheless significant. Once we understand how His universe works, it can be very beneficial as we work with God in establishing His Kingdom here on earth.

The words we speak hold power over ourselves and others. As followers of Christ, we must bring this principle in line with God's Word and practice it carefully.

Reflect on the following Scripture verses and write it into a personal statement.

Proverbs 18:20-22 (NKJ)
A man's stomach shall be satisfied from the fruit of his mouth, from the produce of his lips he shall be filled. Death and life are in the power of the tongue, and those who love it will eat its fruit.

_____

_____

_____

James 3:5-6 (NKJ)
Even so the tongue is a little member and boasts great things. See how great a forest a little fire kindles! And the tongue is a fire, a world of iniquity. The tongue is set among our members that it defiles the whole body, and sets on fire the course of nature; and it is set on fire by hell.

_____

_____

Day 3

My desire is for you to see God's principles in action and to experience His rich provision in your life. When you start functioning within these principles, your life will become rich through His Word and His presence. They become a protective and blessed framework you can operate in and you will soon see the results in your life.

Review today's lesson.

1. Prayerfully choose one statement or verse that was most meaningful to you today.

_____

_____

_____

2. Write a prayer of response.

_____

_____

_____

3. What action do you need to take in response to today's lesson?

_____

_____

_____

POWER POINTS
- God governs the universe by the Word of His mouth.
- God established the laws of multiplication through seedtime and harvest.
- God's Word is a solid foundation on which to build.
- When you live according to God's principles, your life will become rich through His Word and His presence.
- The words we speak hold power over ourselves and others.

Journal

Dear friend, I pray that you may enjoy good health and that all may go well with you, even as your soul is getting along well.

3 JOHN 2 (NIV)

MYTHS CONCERNING SOVEREIGNTY AND PROSPERITY

Perhaps we see God's Sovereignty from a human prospective only. a human possesses the power of sovereignty he might reserve th right to override his written contract or promises (words) if th outcome does not justify his purpose and plan. He has to change constantl to maintain his purpose and plan to bring about the desired results. Wit human limitations, this may have to be done in order to justify the end result. But God cannot lie. He knows the end from the beginning. When He gave Hi Word to us as a guide to live our life, He limited Himself within that Word. Hi written Word is full of His expressions of limitations.

Job 38:4-13 (NKJ)

Where were you when I laid the foundations of the earth? Tell Me, if you hav understanding. Who determined its measurements? Surely you know! Or who stretche the line upon it? To what were its foundations fastened? Or who laid its cornerston. when the morning stars sang together, and all the sons of God shouted for joy? Or wh shut in the sea with doors, when it burst forth and issued from the womb; when I maa the clouds its garment, and thick darkness its swaddling band; when I fixed My lim for it, and set bars and doors; when I said, `This far you may come, but no farthe. and here your proud waves must stop! Have you commanded the morning since you days began, and caused the dawn to know its place, that it might take hold of the en. of the earth, and the wicked be shaken out of it?

However, I believe that within that limit He has unlimited avenues and unlimited ways to accomplish His purpose without violating His written Word and overturning His promises. I also believe that He has given us the ability to access all those unlimited avenues through Jesus Christ. Our human mind, however, is not able to fathom His unlimited limitation. How can a mortal man ever understand an immortal God?

Why do you think God put Himself under such limitations?

_____

_____

_____

His passionate love for the human soul created those boundaries. He loved us so much that He gave us Himself to save us from the bondage of sin. I believe He limited His wrath (anger) and judgment also.

God is all love, perfectly Holy, totally just and He created us. We will not be able to fathom how all those attributes of God work together to save us and love us.

He gave us His Word. He will bless us within the boundaries of that Word. He will judge us according to the boundaries of that Word. His Word contains two important things: God's facts and God's promises. God's facts are past and have to be believed and trusted. All the promises are in the future tense and they are conditional. To take advantage of those promises a person has to fulfill the conditions in order to reap the benefits. Promises are given so we can live effectively now and to receive our reward in eternity. You cannot attain those promises little by little, but you have to obtain them by faith.

Hebrews 11:6
But without faith it is impossible to please Him, for he who comes to God must believe that He is, and that He is a rewarder of those who diligently seek Him.

Knowledge about God

As Christians we believe:

- God is the Creator of the heavens and earth.
- He provides us our daily food, sunshine, air to breathe and rules over the Universe.
- He has given us the written Word and revealed Himself through that Word.

- He planned and sent Jesus for our redemption.
- God is Triune. There are three persons in the Godhead: the Father, the Son and the Holy Spirit. All three work together to bring the plan of salvation into action in believers' lives.
- Without faith it is impossible to please God. We have to obey and live life according to the Word of God.
- In order to obtain eternal life we need to receive Jesus Christ as our personal Saviour.

This knowledge about God created the Christian religion and culture. However it also brought myths around God. It created a mental distance between Him and us. Somehow—apart from giving God lip service about His sovereign power—for many, God's personality is weak. The sovereign power of God has created an emotional garbage dump for many—Christians and non-Christians alike. The sovereignty of God becomes a "safe"place to dump the undesired results of all our irresponsible behaviour. It creates a comforting pretence and hides those times when we have deliberately chosen to disobey God.

When we, in our ignorance, fail to appropriate God's facts into our lives, we may fall into the trap of explaining our failure as the result of God's sovereignty. When we shift the responsibility to God, rather than acknowledging our own lack of obedience or understanding, we are a poor witness of God's Word. Instead of acting like soldiers of God's Word, we take a certain pride in being "victims" of God's sovereignty. Jesus said, "... the things I do, you will do also and greater things." Still, even when we miss out on the fullness of God's provision, God is merciful and gives us a second chance to rise up in the midst of failure, change our ways and possess our personal promised land.

Knowledge about God stimulates our trust, but knowing God actually establishes our trust in Him, produces faith and brings about temporal and eternal results.

My Story

In my own life, I came to realize that I could not lead a successful life on my own. I wanted to find a reliable, powerful partner who could—and wanted to—be with me. As I searched for someone, I concluded that nobody in the world would do anything without the promise of profit. I turned to the Scriptures and tried to discuss financial matters with experienced, mature Christians, but I couldn't find satisfactory answers there either.

My parents were very good Christians, but they never went to the Scriptures for answers when they experienced financial difficulties. It seemed

to me that, although it was highly acceptable for Christians to be wealthy, it was unacceptable to discuss financial issues. Well-meaning Christians tried to justify a lack of understanding about the material realm and God's part in it, by attributing everything to God's sovereignty. In other words, that we have no control over our own financial affairs, but rather that God decides whether we should be poor or rich or even whether we should just stay where we are and get by.

If prosperity was dependent upon the sovereignty of God, then there was neither reward for following Christ nor penalty for ignoring Christ. And if what I was hearing from others about the sovereignty of God was true, in my opinion that made us mere puppets in His plan. It just did not feel right in my heart. As I searched for the truth in this matter, the Holy Spirit directed me to Scripture and guided me step by step. As I spent time with God and in His Word, I started to change.

Living the Word of God

As my life was developing as a new Christian, I noticed inconsistency between what I was reading in God's Word and what I was seeing in the lives of Christians around me. Concepts like peace were talked about but never lived out. Healing was proclaimed but few received it from God. Passages like John 10:10 and 3 John 2 became confusing to me. I was particularly troubled by how many Christians in the church suffered financially.

Too often I was told that everything was under God's Sovereignty. It sounded to me like my faith in His written Word counted very little, but that God's will was final. I could not deny God's sovereignty, but I did question these interpretations and these ways of thinking in my heart. I started to try and bring everything under God's sovereignty alone, even my financial matters which included giving to the church for the sake of spreading of the Gospel. I wondered why giving to the church seemed to depend on my own will, while everything else depended on God's will alone. Things didn't line up for me.

Jesus said that we will know the truth and the truth shall set us free. Our thinking has to be God's thinking. Our observations, associations, and any obstacles we encounter, influence us into forming certain thought-patterns. We must replace our own thoughts with God's thoughts. Jesus' words "If you abide in me and my words abide in you then whatever you will ask, it will be done for you" call for oneness with Him.

In Matthew 6:33 it is written, "But seek first the kingdom of God and His righteousness, and all these things shall be added to you." (NKJ) Take a few moments and consider your own understanding of this verse.

In all honesty, in view of this passage, when I started out, I really did not understand what to believe and what not to believe about my financial matters. My thoughts were clouded with religious thinking. I now realize that I did believe God's truth but only in part—I did not embrace the whole truth.

The Holy Spirit is there to interpret the Word of God, but He will never contradict or go beyond God's Word. There are no new revelations outside God's Word. When we are not well versed in the Word of God, some points of view might appear like new revelations to us , while in reality they have existed in the Bible since the beginning. God's Will for our lives is never automatic; we must participate with Him to bring it to operation in this world.

Review today's lesson.

1. Prayerfully choose one statement or verse that was most meaningful to you today.

_____

_____

2. Write a prayer of response.

_____

_____

3. What action do you need to take in response to today's lesson?

_____

_____

POWER POINTS

- God is sovereign, but He limited Himself, showing mercy to the helpless.
- His Word is the final authority.
- I am to live by the Word, be blessed by the Word and be judged by the Word.
- Knowledge about God stimulates trust.
- Knowing God establishes that trust.
- There are no new revelations outside God's Word.

Journal

_____

_____

_____

_____

_____

_____

_____

_____

_____

_____

_____

_____

_____

_____

_____

_____

_____

_____

_____

_____

_____

_____

_____

_____

_____

_____

_____

_____

_____

_____

_____

_____

_____

_____

_____

_____

_____

_____

_____

_____

_____

TRUSTING THE MASTER FINANCIER

Knowledge of God does not come automatically. It has to be pursued, nurtured and valued. Problems often lead us closer to God or create bitterness towards God. When you know God and the way He is, then nothing can separate us from His love. That is why Paul wrote in Romans 8:35-39: Who shall separate us from the love of Christ? Shall tribulation, or distress, or persecution, or famine, or nakedness, or peril, or sword? As it is written: 'For Your sake we are killed all day long; we are accounted as sheep for the slaughter.' Yet in all these things we are more than conquerors through Him who loved us. For I am persuaded that neither death nor life, nor angels nor principalities nor powers, nor things present nor things to come, nor height nor depth, nor any other created thing, shall be able to separate us from the love of God which is in Christ Jesus our Lord.

God created all by the Word of His mouth. It includes gold, silver, diamonds, and precious stones and He brought the systems of trade, commerce and government to existence. If God had not taught us the difference between gold and iron, we would have not known about it.

He gives wisdom, knowledge and desires. He is the only one who knows how to fulfill those desires. Philippians 2:13 says, "For it is God who works in you both to will and to do for His good pleasure."

We may disqualify all our efforts and progress of all seven sessions in this book by introducing one statement without qualifying it which is: God is sovereign and ultimately the results lie in Him.

What is your opinion about the sovereign position of God?

_____

_____

_____

_____

_____

> ## Who shall separate us from the love of Christ?
>
> ROMANS 8:35

God is sovereign. He cannot be more righteous or less righteous. He is eternal, sovereign, omnipotent, omnipresent and omniscient. He is all love and at the same time He is an absolutely just judge. He is all good, all kind and all merciful and He cannot tolerate sin at all. Advocating God's goodness through our human mind and words cannot make Him more holy.

Somehow, if we do not bring out God's sovereignty and give Him all the responsibility for our failures, then it weakens God's power in our mind.

Can we really explain God? Job was a righteous man; even God said that. Job tried to find reasons why he got into trouble but found himself in turmoil and pain. (Read Job 38-40 for a clear exposition of God's sovereignty.) God expects us to understand, act, believe, trust and build our faith on His Word.

He has created us with limitations, and it is impossible for us to know His limitless power and ability. He wants us to know Him and trust Him within those limitations. He put Himself under the same limits and boundaries at one time. Jesus came only for a limited period. He only did a limited number of works. He gives us limited years on this earth to know Him.

God's Word describes His boundaries. For us, nothing—absolutely nothing—goes beyond the Word of God and nothing happens to us outside of God's Word. Every revelation, vision, prophecy, word of knowledge, word of wisdom, dream and teaching must stay and abide by the written Word of God. There is no new knowledge outside the Word of God and there won't be any until Jesus comes.

Boundaries:

Ecclesiastes 5:18-19

Here is what I have seen: It is good and fitting for one to eat and drink, and to enjoy the good of all his labor in which he toils under the sun all the days of his life which God gives him; for it is his heritage. As for every man to whom God has given riches and wealth, and given him power to eat of it, to receive his heritage and rejoice in his labor this is the gift of God.

_____

_____

Ecclesiastes 6:1-2

There is an evil which I have seen under the sun, and it is common among men: A man to whom God has given riches and wealth and honor, so that he lacks nothing for himself of all he desires; yet God does not give him power to eat of it, but a foreigner consumes it. This is vanity, and it is an evil affliction.

_____

_____

God gave us His Word so that we may trust Him and enlarge our faith in His faithfulness.

When God's Word continuously leads us to trust Him, do you think we should trust in His written Word or His Sovereignty? Explain.

_____

_____

_____

_____

_____

_____

God's Word holds us accountable and challenges our faith. We are to live by His Word and act by His Word—our whole life should be governed by His Word. We will also be judged according to His Word.

John 1:1
In the beginning was the Word, and the Word was with God, and the Word was God.

It is easy to live life without any accountability if we consider God's sovereignty over His Word. God's sovereignty or involvement in our lives does not negate our free will, the principle of sowing and reaping, or our hunger and thirst for a personal relationship with Him.

Review today's lesson.
1. Prayerfully choose one statement or verse that was most meaningful to you today.

_____

_____

_____

_____

_____

_____

2. Write a prayer of response.

_____

_____

_____

_____

_____

_____

_____

_____

3. What action do you need to take in response to today's lesson?

_____

_____

_____

_____

_____

POWER POINTS

■ God is sovereign and worthy of your trust.

■ You can be successful by operating within His written Word.

■ You are accountable for your actions according to His Word.

■ His Word holds everything together.

Day 5

Journal

YOU, GOD AND PROSPERITY

Financial prosperity is a journey, not a destination. Learning God's principles for success and applying them in our lives requires prayer, faith and patience. But once we understand that this is the only way to lasting success, we won't get tired of doing the same thing every day. We will be diligent in prayer. We will strive for excellence and endeavour to improve continuously.

Jesus is the reason we can have success. The redeemed financial life is intimately connected with the spiritual life. First, we need to determine all that God wants to do through us.

Ask yourself, What do you plan to do with your life? What kind of steward should you be? What kind of legacy do you want to leave for your children and grandchildren? Then count the cost.

Each of us has to decide what our lives will accomplish. Depending on your choice, you will either go to high places, or nowhere. It is a choice.

Where are you in your walk with God? Where can you start from today?

_____

_____

Psalm 46:10
Be still, and know that I am God; I will be exalted among the nations, I will be exalted in the earth!

Read Malachi 1: 6-14 and state where you are at in your relationship with God.

_____

_____

> I am the vine; you are the branches. If a man remains in me and I in him, he will bear much fruit; apart from me you can do nothing.
>
> JOHN 15:5 (NIV)

Day 6

Now read Malachi 3:13-15.

"Your words have been harsh against Me," says the LORD, "Yet you say, `What have we spoken against You?' You have said, `It is useless to serve God; what profit is it that we have kept His ordinance, and that we have walked as mourners before the LORD of hosts? So now we call the proud blessed, for those who do wickedness are raised up; they even tempt God and go free."

Ask the Holy Spirit to bring to mind any times you might have thought or said these things. Then ask God for forgiveness.

_____

_____

_____

_____

I have spoken similar words under my breath many times. I was ignorant then, but I have learned my lesson and God in His mercy opened my eyes to see it. He taught me to repent. I cried out to the Lord and He answered me.

Malachi 3: 16-18

Then those who feared the LORD spoke to one another, and the LORD listened and heard them; so a book of remembrance was written before Him for those who fear the LORD and who meditate on His name. 'They shall be Mine,' says the LORD of hosts, 'On the day that I make them My jewels. And I will spare them as a man spares his own son who serves him.' Then you shall again discern between the righteous and the wicked, between one who serves God and one who does not serve Him.

Your Personal Relationship with Christ is a Prerequisite

In this study I shall assume that you have accepted Jesus Christ as your personal Saviour, that you have made Him Lord of your life, and that you are making an effort to walk in the Spirit. When you start walking in the Spirit, you will have spiritual discernment by the indwelling Spirit of Christ in you. Our experience with God leads us to live in freedom, which leads to an abundant life. Our spiritual experience and growth is the key to our success. If you are not sure about your personal relationship with Jesus, however, consider the following four spiritual principles:

1. God loves you and offers a wonderful plan for your life.

2. All of us are sinful and separated from God. Therefore, we cannot know and experience God's love and plan for our lives.

3. Jesus Christ is Gods only provision for our sins. Through Him, we can know

and experience God's love and plan for our lives.

4. We must individually accept Jesus Christ as Savior and Lord; then we can know and experience God's love and His plan for our lives.

(From The Four Spiritual Laws by Bill Bright)

Compare your own life with what the Word of God has to say. Write each Scripture into a statement of faith.

Example: John 1:12

But as many as received Him, to them He gave the right to become children of God, to those who believe in His name

I believe in Your Name and by faith I declare that I am a child of God.

Ephesians 2:8-9

For by grace you have been saved through faith, and that not of yourselves; it is the gift of God, not of works, lest anyone should boast.

_____

_____

_____

John 3:1-8

The wind blows where it wishes, and you hear the sound of it, but cannot tell where it comes from and where it goes. So is everyone who is born of the Spirit.

_____

_____

_____

Revelation 3:20

Behold, I stand at the door and knock. If anyone hears My voice and opens the door, I will come in to him and dine with him, and he with Me.

_____

_____

_____

When you accept Jesus as your personal Saviour you become a child of God and your sins are forgiven. Jesus grants you a new life and He promises not to leave you and forsake you as you pursue the lifestyle laid out in the Word of God—a lifestyle based on total dependency on God.

2 Corinthians 5: 17

Therefore, if anyone is in Christ, he is a new creation; old things have passed away; behold, all things have become new.

_____

_____

_____

_____

When you start this new journey with Jesus you need to experience God's love and forgiveness daily. Being born again is not an event, but it is starting a new experience which will last all throughout your life. Knowing Jesus intimately changes our perspective on finances and leads us into financial freedom.

The amount of money you have has nothing to do with financial security or contentment. Neither can satisfaction be found in wise investments, careful budgets, or debt-free living. Instead, the secret to financial freedom and joy is directly linked to one thing: the willingness to be generous with what you have.

—Author unknown

Matthew 6:33

Seek first the kingdom of God and His righteousness, and all these things shall be added to you.

What does seeking the kingdom of God mean to you?

_____

_____

_____

_____

_____

What steps can you take to ensure that you seek the kingdom of God first in your life?

_____

_____

_____

_____

_____

What are your priorities in life at this moment? Please circle the ones that apply to you.

- ■ To have a good job.
- ■ To have a normal life like most other people.
- ■ To have fun and see the world.
- ■ To have a family and be happy.
- ■ To achieve something big in life.
- ■ To find God's purpose and join Him.

What do you think should your priorities be? List them.

_____

_____

_____

_____

_____

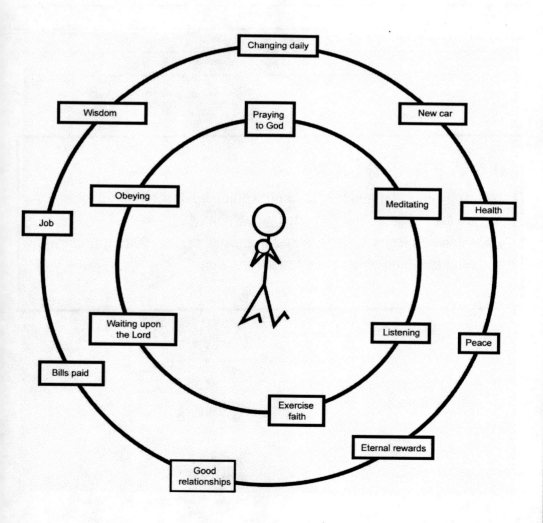

Review today's lesson.

1. Prayerfully choose one statement or verse that was most meaningful to you today.

_____

_____

_____

_____

2. Write a prayer of response.

_____

_____

_____

_____

3. What action do you need to take in response to today's lesson?

_____

_____

_____

_____

POWER POINTS

■ Your financial and personal difficulties lie in the issue of your heart.

■ Knowing Jesus intimately changes your perspective on finances and will lead your into financial freedom.

*J*ournal

Day 7

OBEDIENCE: THE CHOICE IS YOURS

God wants us to be mature and act independently, but in Him. Outside of God we have a very limited capacity to succeed.

Please meditate on these verses today. Let the Holy Spirit breathe truth into your heart.

Deuteronomy 30:19

I call heaven and earth to record this day against you, that I have set before you life and death, blessing and cursing: therefore choose life, that both thou and thy seed may live.

_____

_____

John 15: 7

If you abide in Me, and My words abide in You, You will ask what you desire, and it shall be done for you.

_____

_____

What action is God stirring in your heart?

_____

_____

When God speaks to us by His Word, it warms our hearts and hope flows in. He wants us to respond on a spiritual level, but also practically by taking action. He wants to bless us and prosper us for His own Word's sake.

It is crucial to respond to Him. You respond to Him by believing and obeying His Word. Nothing gives God more pleasure than knowing His children believe in Him. This must be done with a willing heart. A willing heart is a surrendered heart with a renewed mind.

Why do you think God wants to bless you and prosper you? Mark the correct answers.

- ■ So I can live comfortably and enjoy God's grace.
- ■ God is merciful and kind and He just wants me to have His best.
- ■ God is a giver and He gives. I do not have to do anything for Him.
- ■ God can take care of His own work because He can do anything.
- ■ He blesses me so that I will obey Him and be a witness for Him and for His work.

Now explain in your own words why you think God wants to bless you and prosper you.

_____

_____

_____

Review today's lesson.

1. Prayerfully choose one statement or verse that was most meaningful to you today.

_____

_____

_____

2. Write a prayer of response.

_____

_____

_____

_____

_____

_____

In everything that he undertook in the service of God's temple and in obedience to the law and the commands, he sought his God and worked wholeheartedly. And so he prospered.

2 CHRONICLES 31:21

3. What action do you need to take in response to today's lesson?

_____

_____

_____

_____

_____

_____

POWER POINTS
- ■ Outside Of God you have a very limited capacity to succeed.
- ■ You can respond to God by believing and obeying His Word.
- ■ Cultivate a willing heart that submits to God.

 Journal

_____
_____
_____
_____
_____
_____
_____
_____
_____
_____
_____
_____
_____
_____
_____
_____
_____
_____
_____
_____
_____
_____
_____
_____
_____
_____
_____
_____
_____
_____
_____
_____
_____
_____
_____
_____
_____
_____
_____

III

GOD'S PRINCIPLES

> The Lord was with Joseph and he prospered, and he lived in the house of his Egyptian master. When his master saw that the Lord gave him success in everything he did, Joseph found favor in his eyes and became his attendant.
>
> GENESIS 39:2-4

THE BASIC PRINCIPLES OF GOD'S LAW

Why do the ungodly prosper? Probably every Christian considers this question at some point. Not to mention many of the other questions regarding God's blessing, like:

- Why is it that an ungodly person sometimes seems more blessed than a godly one?
- Should a Christian wait patiently to be blessed in eternity and not consider earthly blessings?
- Should a Christian aspire to gain wealth in this world, or not?
- Does it really matter whether a Christian is wealthy, or not?

God has established a set of basic principles by which the earth operates. These principles were designed for the good of mankind.

Reflect on the following Scripture:

Genesis 1:28
Then God blessed them, and God said to them, be fruitful and multiply; fill the earth and subdue it; have dominion over the fish of the sea, over the birds of the air, and over every living thing that moves on the earth.

_____

_____

God established His Law from the very beginning. It is based on His love and His desire to save all. God provides everyone with sunshine, rain and air to breathe. He has put in motion some very specific physical laws to govern our lives. When these physical laws interact with the spiritual laws of God, it produces prosperous life in and around us.

When a person operates solely within the physical law of God, he/she can still prosper in this life. These physical laws affect believers and non-believers equally. God is no respecter of persons. These laws are a gift from God and they work every time a person, regardless of his/her spiritual condition, dares to apply them.

God's Word is full of facts and promises. Distinguish whether the following verses contain a fact or a promise:

Isaiah 1:19-20

If ye be willing and obedient, ye shall eat the good of the land; but if ye refuse and rebel ye shall be devoured with the sword: for the mouth of the LORD hath spoken it.

_____

_____

Deuteronomy 28:1-2

Now it shall come to pass, if you diligently obey the voice of the LORD your God, to observe carefully all His commandments which I command you today, that the Lord your God will set you high above all nations of the earth. And all these blessings shall come upon you and overtake you, because you obey the voice of the LORD your God.

_____

_____

The principle of work

God wants everybody to work. In the beginning when He created Adam, He gave him work to do.

What work did God give Adam to do?

Genesis 2:8, 15

The Lord God planted a garden eastward in Eden, and there He put the man whom He had formed ... Then the Lord God took the man and put him in the Garden of Eden to tend and keep it.

_____

_____

_____

_____

Adam had to look after the Garden of Eden.

What is work according to Ecclesiastes 5: 18 -20 ?

Here is what I have seen: It is good and fitting for one to eat and drink, and to enjoy the good of all his labor in which he toils under the sun all the days of his life, which God gives him; for it is his heritage. As for every man to whom God has given riches and wealth, and given him power to eat of it, to receive his heritage and rejoice in his labor—this is the gift of God. He will not dwell unduly on the days of his life, because God keeps him busy with the joy of his heart."

_____

_____

_____

_____

What does God promise in the following verse?

Deuteronomy 28:12

The Lord will open to you His good treasure, the heavens, to give the rains to your land in its season and to bless all the work of your hand.

_____

_____

_____

_____

God promises to bless the work of our hands. Working is not the world's idea; it is God's principle by which He can bless His people.

What does the New Testament say about work?

1 Thessalonians 4:11-12

That you also aspire to lead a quiet life, to mind your own business, and to work with your own hands, as we commanded you. That you may walk properly toward those who are outside, and that you may lack nothing.

_____

_____

_____

_____

2 Thessalonians 5:10-11

For even when we were with you, we commanded you this: If anyone will not work, neither shall he eat. For we hear that there are some who walk among you in a disorderly manner, not working at all, but are busybodies.

_____

_____

_____

Paul instructed the Christians in Thessalonica not to keep company with persons who didn't work.

What is your attitude towards work?

_____

_____

_____

Whether he was in captivity, or whether he was a slave, Joseph worked in a productive manner. He had a strong work ethic and God blessed him. King David, on the other hand, was idle in a moment he was supposed to be with his army on the battlefield. It was at that time that he committed adultery with Bathsheba. Remember the saying, "an idle mind is the devil's workshop"?

Are there any changes you need to make where you are right now?

_____

_____

_____

Are there any changes you need to make in your place of work?

_____

_____

_____

Ask God to bring to mind any times when you have not been a good and faithful worker. Seek His forgiveness and restoration.

_____

_____

_____

Define God's principle of work in your own words.

_____

_____

_____

Review today's lesson.

1. Prayerfully choose one statement or verse that was most meaningful to you today.

_____

_____

_____

2. Write a prayer of response.

_____

_____

_____

_____

_____

_____

3. What action do you need to take in response to today's lesson?

_____

_____

_____

POWER POINTS

■ Work is God's principle by which He can bless His people.
■ The physical laws of multiplication and seedtime and harvest equally affect believers and non-believers.
■ God's Word contains both facts and promises.

Journal

_____

_____

_____

_____

_____

_____

_____

_____

_____

_____

_____

_____

_____

_____

_____

_____

_____

_____

_____

_____

_____

_____

_____

_____

_____

_____

_____

_____

_____

_____

_____

_____

_____

_____

_____

_____

_____

_____

_____

THE PRINCIPLE OF GUIDANCE

Whoever gives heed to instruction prospers, and blessed is he who trusts in the Lord.

PROVERBS 16: 20. (NIV)

It is essential to increase in knowledge, especially if you lack insight into your own financial affairs. Knowledge is the key to opening the door of your future. Each individual has his own expertise, gifts and areas of knowledge. A person might know how to pray, but might not know the current state of global economics. Similarly, it is most likely a waste of time seeking medical advice from a financial advisor or stock broker. God provides experts who can help guide us when we need answers.

Reflect on the following Scriptures and write them into your own statement:

Proverbs 11:14

Where there is no counsel the people fall: but in the multitude of counselors there is safety.

_____

_____

Proverbs 15:22

Without counsel, plans go awry, but in the multitude of counselors they are established.

_____

_____

Proverbs 12:15

The way of a fool is right in his own eyes, but he who heeds counsel is wise.

_____

_____

_____

Proverbs 19:20

Listen to counsel and receive instruction, that you may be wise in your latter days.

_____

_____

_____

Proverbs 20:5

Counsel in the heart of man is like deep water, but a man of understanding will draw it out.

_____

_____

_____

Proverbs 24: 6

For by wise counsel you will wage your own war. And in a multitude of counselors there is safety.

_____

_____

_____

In a world that is constantly changing, it is impossible to know everything. We need others to help guide us in the affairs of life. God has established this transfer of wisdom from one to another through counsel and guidance. Scripture shows that guidance is not man's invention, but God's idea. He asked kings to take counsel from the wise both in running their countries and in times of war.

Do you know any financial experts? Write down the name of one person you might consult about your finances.

_____

_____

_____

Perhaps you might think that you do not have much money to talk about and feel intimidated by financially knowledgeable people. Everyone has to start somewhere. What you need is a plan and probably a little bit of guidance. As you learn God's principles for redeeming your finances, your small amounts may become like the five loaves of bread and two fish in the hand of the Master, the chief Financial Planner.

There are a number of ways you may increase your financial knowledge:

- Contact a financial advisor today.
- Go to financial seminars in your area.
- Try and keep up with current events that affect your financial status.

Take some time to get a good understanding of the basics of handling your finances. Here are some key concepts every one of us needs to know:

- How do you balance a checkbook?

- How do you do banking through Interac, telephone and the Internet?

- Where will you earn the most interest?

- What options do you have for savings on travel?

- What is a bond?

- What is the money market?

- What are securities?

- What are stocks?

- How can you pay less tax, instead of more?

- What are tax shelter privileges?

- What is an RRSP?

- What is an RESP?

A special word to women

Proverbs 31 encourages women to be involved in business while taking care of their family. I am encouraged by how many women take an interest in their financial affairs. Still, too many women depend solely on their husbands to take care of finances and do not pay any attention to investments. God's Word states clearly that man and woman are joint partners on earth. I believe that man and woman are equally responsible for taking care of their financial affairs. (Besides, two viewpoints are generally better than one.)

Ask a mentor

Experts suggest that we should update our financial affairs every year. Do this with someone who is knowledgeable—like a financial mentor. Such a mentor should be someone who is doing well financially. You probably won't learn much from someone who still struggles with the same financial issues you do. Always try and learn from someone who is further along the road than you are.

Don't try and shove your financial struggles in a secret closet. The more we try and hide from these problems, the larger they tend to become. When you deal with them, you might experience freedom sooner than you think.

Who are you accountable to for your financial affairs?

_____

_____

_____

God's plans versus our plans

We must always desire God's guidance first, even when choosing a financial mentor. Understanding what God is about to do in your life—right where you are—is more important than telling God how to fix your problem. God prepares us internally first; then He deals with our external circumstances. He knows that if our hearts are not renewed and fixed first, we will eventually go back to our old habits. God's plan for you is always larger than your circumstances.

God had a plan for Moses. His instruction started in Pharoah's house and continued during the 40 years in the wilderness. As soon as Moses was ready, God made him a ruler over His own people.

God promised Abraham that he would be the father of many nations and would have all the land his eyes could see. God had to build his character first, however, and Abraham waited 99 years before receiving his promised son.

David was trained by the Holy Spirit in the wilderness while tending sheep. He learned to fight lions and bears before he had to face Goliath. He learned to fight for his life and win battles in spite of strong opposition. All the while, God was preparing a man after His own heart.

Although 13-year old Joseph's dream foretold of a future where he would be a leader, even over his own family, he faced more troubles than either you or I could care for. Still, Joseph never complained. God was preparing Joseph for his task.

Queen Esther was prepared for a specific task. She had to be obedient and save the Jews.

Perhaps God is preparing you for some future task. You are the only one who can choose to stay in the Potter's Hand and allow Him to turn you into a vessel of joy and contentment.

Ask God today to mould your life into the beautiful vessel He has in mind.

_____

_____

_____

_____

_____

List the things you can (and need to) change and those things only God can do for you.

_____

_____

_____

_____

_____

Frequently we want God to bless us, yet we are not prepared to change. When God moves in your life, start making the necessary adjustments. When He moves, He is ready to come to your situation and bless you.

Meditate on the following Scripture:

Psalm 1:1-4

Blessed is the man who walks not in the counsel of the ungodly, nor stands in the path of sinners, nor sits in the seat of the scornful; but his delight is in the law of the LORD, and in His law he meditates day and night. He shall be like a tree planted by the rivers *of water, that brings forth its fruit in its season, whose leaf also shall not wither; and whatever he does shall prosper.*

_____

_____

_____

Review today's lesson.

1. Prayerfully choose one statement or verse that was most meaningful to you today.

_____

_____

_____

2. Write a prayer of response.

_____

_____

_____

3. What action do you need to take in response to today's lesson?

_____

_____

_____

POWER POINTS

- It's impossible to know everything.
- Guidance is God's idea.
- Always desire God's guidance first; then look to an expert.
- God's plan for you is always larger than your current circumstances.

*J*ournal

THE PRINCIPLE OF DILIGENCE

The soul of a lazy man desires and has nothing; but the soul of the diligent shall be made rich.

PROVERBS 13:4

Diligent people work carefully. They are usually blessed with wisdom, whether they are believers or unbelievers. With the godly, however, God will direct their paths and if they are in tune with God, they will receive more wisdom. God will bless the work of their hands according to His Word.

Reflect on the following Scriptures and write them into your own statement:

Proverbs 10:4-5

He who has a slack hand becomes poor, but the hand of the diligent makes rich. He who gathers in summer is a wise son; he who sleeps in harvest is a son who causes shame.

_____

_____

A diligent person keeps the door open for blessings from God and from man. She creates opportunities to be promoted and blessed.

Joseph's own brothers mistreated him and sold him to Midianite traders who sold him to Potiphar, an officer in Pharaoh's army. Joseph never complained about his circumstances; but his relationship with God remained constant. He gave God first place in his heart, in good times or bad.

Genesis 39:1-6 (TLB)

When Joseph arrived in Egypt as a captive of the Ishmaelite traders, he was purchased from them by Potiphar, a member of the personal staff of Pharaoh, the king of Egypt. Now this man Potiphar was the captain of the kings bodyguard and his chief executioner. The Lord greatly blessed Joseph there in the home of his master, so that

everything he did succeeded. Potiphar noticed this and realized that the Lord was with Joseph in a very special way. So Joseph naturally became quite a favorite with him. Soon he was put in charge of the administration of Potiphars household, and all of his business affairs. At once the Lord began blessing Potiphar for Josephs sake. All his household affairs began to run smoothly, his crops flourished and his flocks multiplied. So Potiphar gave Joseph the complete administrative responsibility over everything he owned. He hadn't a worry in the world with Joseph there, except to decide what he wanted to eat! Joseph, by the way, was a very handsome young man.

Explain in your own words the results of God's favour in Joseph's life.

_____

_____

_____

_____

_____

In Genesis, Joseph experienced 39 setbacks, including being falsely accused and thrown into prison.

Genesis 39:21 -23 (TLB)

But the Lord was with Joseph there, too, and was kind to him by granting him favor with the chief jailer. In fact, the jailer soon handed over the entire prison administration to Joseph, so that all the other prisoners were responsible to him. The chief jailer had no more worries after that, for Joseph took care of everything, and the Lord was with him so that everything ran smoothly and well."

Diligent people are usually sincere, creative and caring. They are often enterprising and find ways to accomplish tasks more effectively. Diligent people are also attentive to details and take good care of their business affairs.

Proverbs 21:5

The plans of the diligent lead surely to plenty.

_____

_____

_____

Proverbs 22:29

Do you see a man who excels in his work? He will stand before kings; he will not stand before unknown men.

_____

_____

_____

Proverb 12: 24

The hand of the diligent will rule.

_____

_____

_____

Proverbs 27:23-27

Be diligent to know the state of your flocks, and attend to your herds; for riches are not forever, nor does a crown endure to all generations. When the hay is removed, and the tender grass shows itself, and the herbs of the mountains are gathered in, the lambs will provide your clothing, and the goats the price of a field; You shall have enough goats milk for your food, for the food of your household, and the nourishment of your maidservants.

_____

_____

_____

What are the advantages of being a diligent person?

_____

_____

_____

What does it mean to you to be a diligent person?

_____

_____

_____

The *Oxford Canadian Dictionary* defines a diligent person as someone who is careful and steady in work; someone who shows care and effort.

Consider some of the following ideas for being more diligent:

- Work carefully.
- Show care and effort.
- Don't compare yourself with other employees.

■ Don't complain unnecessarily.

■ Find a good purpose in everything you do.

■ Accept correction without resentment.

■ Be patient in doing your best in the sight of God

Are you working where God wants you to work? Ask God to reveal to you His will and perfect plan for your life.

_____

_____

_____

Reflect on your attitude regarding your present job? Ask God to reveal anything out of place and correct it.

_____

_____

_____

Are you indispensable at work? Why or why not?

_____

_____

_____

Do you know anyone who is diligent? Why would you say is this person diligent?

_____

_____

_____

How could you be more diligent at work?

_____

_____

_____

Review today's lesson.

1. Prayerfully choose one statement or verse that was most meaningful to you today.

_____

_____

_____

_____

_____

SESSION 3
Day 3

2. Write a prayer of response.

_____

_____

_____

_____

_____

_____

_____

_____

_____

_____

_____

3. What action do you need to take in response to today's lesson?

_____

_____

_____

POWER POINTS

- ■ God looks favourably upon diligence.
- ■ A diligent person is sincere, creative and caring.
- ■ A diligent person is often an entrepreneur and finds ways to accomplish tasks more effectively.

Journal

THE PRINCIPLE OF KNOWLEDGE

Knowledge is a key element for a life of success. The best kind of knowledge is godly knowledge. There is no failure with God.

God said in Hosea 4:6, "My people are destroyed for lack of knowledge." Most successful people are very knowledgeable in their fields of work. Knowledge has to be acquired and it usually brings progress. We often find that the world pursues knowledge and operates well in this godly principle. Everyone who applies this principle of pursuing knowledge receives its benefit. God gives rain and sunshine to all for their substance so that they might see the fingerprint of God in the universe.

Ecclesiastes 7:12 (NIV)

Wisdom is a shelter as money is a shelter, but the advantage of knowledge is this: that wisdom preserves the life of its possessor.

The Edge

Proverbs 1:1-7

The proverbs of Solomon the son of David, king of Israel: to know wisdom and instruction, to perceive the words of understanding, to receive the instruction of wisdom, justice, judgment, and equity; to give prudence to the simple, to the young man knowledge and discretion. A wise man will hear and increase learning, and a man of understanding will attain wise counsel, to understand a proverb and an enigma, the words of the wise and their riddles. The fear of the LORD is the beginning of knowledge, but fools despise wisdom and instruction.

God wants to bless us and whenever He puts a desire in our hearts to receive further training or take a course, it will improve our situation. Study is hard work, and requires discipline, time and effort.

My people are destroyed for lack of knowledge. Because you have rejected knowledge, I also will reject you from being priest for Me; because you have forgotten the law of your God, I also will forget your children.

HOSEA 4:6

109

Do you ever feel like you have missed opportunities to study or learn more?

_____

If the answer is yes, you may have to ask God to forgive you. Spend a moment in quiet reflection and prayer.

_____
_____
_____

God's leading in these areas of our lives is very personal and practical. Gaining knowledge does not necessarily mean a new university degree–you will have to listen to His unique prompting and direction for your life. In times of economic change, the Spirit might prompt you to take a training program, to change your line of work or to update your educational training. God knows our future and His plans are to prosper us, not harm us.

Is God perhaps speaking to you right now? What is He saying?

_____
_____
_____

Ultimately, whether you listen and respond to the promptings of the Holy Spirit is entirely up to you. When people who don't know God make decisions based on common sense, we call it a sensible approach. Christians may also be sensible. But in a world that is constantly changing, it is even more important for every Christian to pay undivided attention to that inner voice of God.

Knowledge can be destructive outside of God. God displays His knowledge all around us. The fear of the Lord is the beginning of wisdom. Wisdom is the principled thing. In the book of Proverbs, Solomon, the wisest man who ever lived, advised us to pursue wisdom and love.

J.I. Packer wrote in his book _Knowing God_: "We ask again: what does it mean for God to give us wisdom? What kind of a gift is it? To live wisely you have to be clear-sighted and realistic—ruthlessly so—in looking at life as it is. Wisdom will not go with comforting illusions, false sentiment, or the use of rose-colored spectacles."

As children, when we are encouraged to go to school and learn, we are making our ways prosperous. On the other hand, when we don't pursue any kind of education, we harm our future prosperity. Parents have a responsibility to guide and mentor their children, to help develop their skills and abilities.

This does not mean that everyone has to pursue a PhD. Since we all have different skills and talents, we can strive to be skilled in the areas of our interest. The opportunities for improvement around us are vast. Lack of knowledge is our own enemy.

Reflect on the following Scriptures and write them as a statement or a prayer.

Psalm 19:1-2
The heavens declare the glory of God; and the firmament shows His handiwork. Day unto day utters speech night unto night reveals knowledge.

_____

_____

Psalm 119:66
Teach me good judgments and knowledge.

_____

_____

Proverbs 1:5
A wise man will hear and increase learning.

_____

_____

Psalm 119:66
Wise people store up knowledge, but the mouth of the foolish is near destruction.

_____

_____

Proverbs 12: 1
Whoever loves instruction loves knowledge, but he who ever hates instruction is stupid.

_____

_____

Proverbs 24:3-4

Through wisdom a house is built, and by understanding it is established; by knowledge the rooms are filled with all precious and pleasant riches.

_____

_____

Proverbs 20:15.

It is written: "There is gold and a multitude of rubies, but the lips of knowledge are a precious jewels."

_____

_____

When we learn to operate with God's wisdom, we will start to operate in God's law and experience the benefits.

Are you operating in the godly principle of knowledge? Explain how you are doing it.

_____

_____

_____

Prepare a plan by which to take concrete action in acquiring knowledge.

_____

_____

_____

_____

_____

_____

_____

_____

_____

_____

_____

_____

Review today's lesson.

1. Prayerfully choose one statement or verse that was most meaningful to you today.

_____

_____

_____

_____

2. Write a prayer of response.

_____

_____

_____

_____

_____

_____

_____

_____

_____

3. What action do you need to take in response to today's lesson?

_____

_____

_____

POWER POINTS

- Lack of knowledge is your enemy.
- God will guide you uniquely in gaining further knowledge.
- Responding to the promptings of the Holy Spirit is always a choice.
- Knowledge and education are tools by which God can make us prosperous.

*J*ournal

THE PRINCIPLE OF PATIENCE

It takes nine months for a baby to grow in the mother's womb. It takes years and years of patience for a parent to see that same baby grow up to be a responsible adult.

When we plant a seed, it takes days to sprout. A farmer works patiently on his field to get a good crop at the end of the season. Storm and rain come and sometimes the farmer has to work through inclement weather, disease, insects and fungus. He still expects to reap a harvest, however.

No matter what kind of profession we are in, we are not exempt from the principle of seedtime and harvest. Whether at work or at home, as a mother and wife, I am subject to the same principle.

Our financial investment is a slow process; it takes time for money to grow. Be aware of the false principle of making fast money. Fast money is not God's principle, but seedtime and harvest is. Satan, your enemy, will try to counteract this principle by making impatience control your life and bring about financial disaster.

Saving takes a long time. It requires patience on the part of a person to leave his or her money in a spot to grow. It takes knowledge and prudence to put the money in a proper investment. It also takes proper investigation to find out which field of work is in demand in your lifetime and how to take full advantage of that field. Do not spend the money before income is in your hand, because you do not know what unforeseen event might await you. Do not pursue pleasure, but rather plan for the future.

> Therefore be patient, brethren, until the coming of the Lord. See how the farmer waits for the precious fruit of the earth, waiting patiently for it until it receives the early and latter rain. You also be patient.
>
> JAMES 5:7-8

Proverbs 14:29

A patient man has great understanding.

According to the above verse, what comes with patience?

How patient are you?

_____

_____

_____

Can you recall a time recently when you were particularly patient or impatient? What happened?

_____

_____

_____

Examples of patience

Abraham

Abraham inherited Canaan, received his promised son and became a friend of God by being patient and believing in God and His Word. He had to wait a hundred years to receive his promised son. (You may want to read Genesis12-23 again to appreciate the patience of Abraham.)

Jacob

Jacob had to work 14 years for Laban before he could receive Rachel as his bride. His wealth, however, increased with patience. Because he was patient and had faith in God, he was able to go back to his homeland and be reconciled with his brother. (Read Genesis 29-31.)

Joseph

Joseph had a dream from God when he was only 13. Through all kinds of persecution, even by his own family, he had to wait patiently for his dream to be fulfilled. Patience and faith in God brought him to his God ordained place. (Read Genesis 37-41.)

David

Samuel anointed David when he was only 13 years old. David had to wait many years before he could receive the kingdom God had promised him. He had to be patient with Saul and with himself. He did not take the matter into his own hands but rather waited for God's timing. He had faith in God and His promises. (Read 1 Samuel 16-31.)

Examples of impatience:

Saul

Saul lost his kingdom because he was impatient with Samuel. After winning the war against the Philistines, Saul was supposed to wait for Samuel to come give the sacrifice to the Lord. Samuel said he would come in seven days but was late. Saul's impatience drove him to take on the role of priest and give sacrifice to the Lord. It was not the ordinance of the Lord. So God rejected him and took the kingdom from him and gave it to David. (Read 1 Samuel 13.)

Samson

Samson lost his life by being impatient. (Read Judges13-16)

Abraham Lincoln

He failed as a businessman—as a storekeeper. He failed as a farmer—in fact, he despised this work. He failed in his first attempt to obtain political office. When elected to the legislature he failed when he sought the office of speaker. He failed in his first attempt to go to Congress. He failed when he sought the appointment to the United States Land Office. He failed when he ran for the United States Senate. He failed when his friends sought nomination for the Vice-Presidency on his behalf in 1856.

Many discoveries are made through patience and faith at work. Many wars have been won through patience. Having faith in the living God and developing patience may cause the world to be under our feet. As children of God we often miss out on our heritage because of our impatient nature.

Developing patience depends entirely on you. It cannot be taught in school, it cannot be bought and it cannot be implanted through surgery. It has to be worked out in your own life through practice. Practice your patience daily and it will surely grow. Then, in the midst of difficult situations you may just discover how patient you are.

Pause and ask the Holy Spirit to remind you of a time when you were at your lowest point of patience. Write it on the bottom of this page, pray and pay careful attention to implementing new patience in your life.

_____

_____

_____

The only way to be a winner

Reflect on the following Scriptures and write them into your own statements:

Hebrews 6: 12

... that you do not become sluggish, but imitate those who through faith and patience inherit the promises.

_____

_____

_____

Ecclesiastes 7:8

The end of a thing is better than its beginning; the patient in spirit is better than the proud in spirit.

_____

_____

_____

James 5:7-8

Therefore be patient, brethren, until the coming of the Lord. See how the farmer waits for the precious fruit of the earth, waiting patiently for it until it receives the early and latter rain. You also be patient. Establish your hearts, for the coming of the Lord is at hand.

_____

_____

_____

_____

Review today's lesson.

1. Prayerfully choose one statement or verse that was most meaningful to you today.

_____

_____

_____

_____

2. Write a prayer of response.

_____

_____

_____

_____

_____

3. What action do you need to take in response to today's lesson?

_____

_____

_____

POWER POINTS

- ■ Patience takes time.
- ■ Money and financial assets take time to grow.
- ■ Making fast money is a false principle.
- ■ You may lose out on the fullness of God's blessing when you are impatient.

ESSION **IV**

SEED AND HARVEST

THE IMPORTANCE OF SEEDS

Now he who supplies seed to the sower and bread for food will also supply and increase your store of seed and will enlarge the harvest of your righteousness.

2 CORINTHIANS 9:10 (NIV)

Nearly everything in this world starts with a seed. God established the principle of seedtime and harvest at the creation of the earth and seeds are its most basic element. Since nothing multiplied by nothing remains nothing, you need to sow something in order for God to work and increase your harvest. Even when it seems like you have nothing, ask God to show you which seeds you can sow in order for Him to bless you. When you plant a seed, it grants God access to bless and increase you.

Joe's story

While I was still in the early stages of learning the principle of seedtime and harvest, someone told me the following true story.

Joe found himself in a critical financial situation. Although he diligently looked through the papers and applied to every possible opportunity, he couldn't find a job. He came to the point where he couldn't do anything to change his own situation. Finally he turned to God for counsel. Soon after, he heard about the principle of seeds and the connection of seeds to tithing.

He heard the teaching through some televangelist and it turned him off because of the stigma attached to such evangelists. But he searched the Word of God and the Holy Spirit also led him to some testimonies in Christian magazines. He decided to take a chance and try his fate with God. He was in such dire straits, he had nothing to lose.

Joe prayed and asked God to provide him some seeds he could sow. He waited for God to answer him. One day in this desperate situation he was standing and praying near his window, and the Holy Spirit spoke to him as a strong impression in his heart. He said, "Look, there's some seed." His eyes were opened and he saw his zucchini plant full of zucchinis. He believed in his heart, so he picked zucchinis from his plant and took it to church. At the church he found some cars that weren't locked and he put them in the cars. People didn't know who was doing this strange thing and started locking their cars.

But Joe was determined to fully understand God's principle of harvest. He watered the seeds he had sown with prayer and thanksgiving. Six months later he got a job as a carpet salesperson.

This was a commissioned job and his paycheck depended on sales. For the first few months he received "no" from every customer he visited. He thanked God for every no, and also thanked God for this opportunity to work. He took the opportunity as a seed and at the end of the year he became the top salesperson in the region.

His attitude towards the Word of God and his simple child-like faith, gave him the miracle he needed so desperately. God honoured His obedience and His faith.

What seeds did Joe sow?

_____

_____

_____

Joe's heart was set on God as he diligently sought His truth and His ways. While it might have seemed silly to him to give away zucchinis, he believed that the Holy Spirit had directed him. He obeyed, added faith to his actions and God honoured this. Hebrews 11:6 says, "But without faith it is impossible to please Him, for he who comes to God must believe that He is, and that He is a rewarder of those who diligently seek Him."

What seeds can you begin to sow? If you don't know, ask the Holy Spirit to open your eyes and show you the seeds that are in your hand. Write down anything the Holy Spirit brings to mind.

_____

_____

_____

Proverbs 10:22
The blessing of the LORD makes one rich, and He adds no sorrow with it.

What does it mean to you that God adds no sorrow to His blessings?

_____

Day 1

How does this differ from the world's way of blessing?

_____

_____

_____

Is there anything that stands in your way right now of trusting God and His will for your life? Bring your fears to the Lord, even your doubts. Be honest before God. He knows your heart. Ask the Lord to show you how you can begin walking with Him today.

_____

_____

_____

Review today's lesson.

1. Prayerfully choose one statement or verse that was most meaningful to you today.

_____

_____

_____

_____

_____

2. Write a prayer of response.

_____

_____

_____

_____

_____

_____

_____

_____

_____

3. What action do you need to take in response to today's lesson?

_____

_____

_____

POWER POINTS

- Seeds are the most basic element of the seed and harvest principle.
- You need to sow something in order for God to work and increase your harvest.
- When you plant a seed, it grants God access to bless and increase you.
- God adds no sorrow to His blessings.

THE PRINCIPLE OF PLANTING SEEDS

Planting seeds is the most basic principle of the harvest. Without seed in the ground, there can be no harvest. Farmers know that they cannot expect a crop without first planting the appropriate seed. As Jesus explained in the parable of the Sower, unless the seed of the Word of God is sown, we cannot expect the harvest of salvation. The principle of seed and harvest is a Kingdom principle and it also applies to finances.

Reflect on the following Scriptures:

Proverbs 11:18
The wicked man does deceptive work, but he who sows righteousness will have a sure reward.

_____

_____

Job 4:8
Even as I have seen, those who plow iniquity and sow trouble reap the same.

_____

_____

Hosea 10:12a;13a
Sow for yourself righteousness; reap in mercy ... You have plowed wickedness, you have reaped iniquity. You have eaten the fruit of lies, because you trusted in your own way.

_____

_____

_____

Do not be deceived, God is not mocked; for whatever a man sows, that he will also reap. For he who sows to his flesh will of the flesh reap corruption, but who sows to the Spirit will of the Spirit reap everlasting life.

GALATIANS 6: 7-8

Day 2

Whatever you give becomes seed for God to multiply back for the purpose of blessing His children and meeting needs. Your giving may consist of talents, time, love, kind words, compassion or good works. Since money represents your talent, labour, time, wisdom and choices, the giving of money is really the giving of yourself. Wherever you plant, it will produce the same kind in many different shapes and forms. You should remember that seed always produces after its kind.

The qualities of seeds

• Seeds produce after their own kind.

When you plant apple seeds, eventually you will harvest apples. When you sow righteousness and kind words, you will experience righteousness and receive kind words. Unfortunately, in the same way, when we sow wickedness, harsh words or lies, they, too, come back.

• Plant good seed to receive a good yield.

In *Diligent in Business*, Bob Toms explains that a corn on the cob has about 800 corns on it, with about five cobs to one plant. That is a return of almost 4,000 to one. The Bible, on the other hand, promises a multiplication of 30, 60 or a hundred times when we sow God's Word seed. (See Mark 4:8)

• Seeds need water, sun and good soil in order to grow.

When you plant seeds in the spiritual realm, water them with prayer and affirmations from the Word of God and add faith. Make sure that you sow into good soil, eg. tithing into the Body of Christ, a church, organization or body where the whole gospel is preached.

• Seeds have to die in order to bring forth a harvest of the same kind.

When God created us, He deposited seeds in us which means that we have the capacity to produce. Without planting those seeds in good soil, however, we will not receive our harvest. The first seed is our life. We must plant it to receive life. Christ set the example when He became the Seed. He died in order to impart Life to anyone who would receive it. Galatians 2:20 says, "I have been crucified with Christ, it is no longer I who live, but Christ lives in me; and the life which I now live in the flesh I live by faith in the Son of God, who loved me and gave Himself for me." We receive Life, abundant and eternal, when we die to ourselves.

Giving of yourself

od does not want your money. He really wants you. When Jesus spoke of
"giving that you might receive," He meant money, yes, but He also included
many other important forms of giving. You should give of yourself as seed—
your soul, spirit and body—for God to use, renew, and replenish. Love, concern
for others, time, patience, an encouraging word, even a "good morning" to
your co-worker can all constitute seeds.

ou can start by:

- Firstly, giving yourself to God
- Then you start giving your earnings.
- Your time
- Your concern for others
- Your love
- Your faith, etc.

ake a list of all the different kinds of seed you can sow.

_____

_____

_____

ow make a list of your planned harvest. (What would you like to eap in your life?)

_____

_____

_____

_____

_____

_____

_____

hat kinds of seed would it take to bring forth your planned arvest?

_____

_____

_____

_____

Matthew 6:33 says "But seek first the kingdom of God and His righteousness, and all these things shall be added to you." How does your planned harvest compare with Jesus' words above?

_____

_____

_____

Put God first as the Source of all your supply, and give as seed that which He will multiply back. You are a walking seed bag. In fact, 1 Corinthians 15:38 says, "But God gives it a body as He pleases, and to each seed its own body." God's Word should always be the foundation for your faith and action. Although we do not understand how it starts working, we know that the miracle-working power is in the seed. With God as your Source and your Multiplier, you cannot lose.

Review today's lesson.

1. Prayerfully choose one statement or verse that was most meaningful to you today.

_____

_____

_____

2. Write a prayer of response.

_____

_____

_____

_____

_____

_____

_____

_____

_____

_____

3. What action do you need to take in response to today's lesson?

_____

_____

_____

POWER POINTS

- Seed-planting is the most basic principle of the harvest.
- Without seeds in the ground there can't be a harvest.
- Seed produces after its own kind.
- Seeds have to die in order to bring forth a harvest.

Journal

ADD FAITH: THE MIRACLE-WORKING POWER IS IN THE SEED

God's natural law of seedtime and harvest works for everybody in the world and operates regardless of a person's belief system. But what gives God's children an edge above unbelievers, is faith in Him and His Word. The miracle is activated by faith. Faith in God is the principal thing.

In Mark 11: 22-25 Jesus underlines the importance and power of faith. "I tell you the truth, if anyone says to this mountain, go, throw yourself into the sea, and does not doubt in his heart but believes that what he says will happen, it will be done for him. Therefore I tell you, whatever you ask for in prayer, believe that you have received it, and it will be yours. And when you stand praying, if you hold anything against anyone, forgive him, so that your Father in heaven may forgive you your sins."

Hebrews 11:6 says, "But without faith it is impossible to please Him, for he who comes to God must believe that He is, and that He is a rewarder of those who diligently seek Him."

Your seed can produce an abundant harvest when it is charged with faith in God. The very nature of the seed is that it dies first and only then will it produce plenty. Your seed is always the door out of your troubles. It is anything you do or give to help another person. Your seed is anything that improves the life of someone near you. It may be seed of information, seed of encouragement, seed of love, seed of time, or even the seed of finances. Whatever you plant, you must plant it with faith. Faith gives life to that seed and it will produce and keep your focus on the Word of God. Start viewing your

This is what the kingdom of God is like. A man scatters seed on the ground. Night and day, whether he sleeps or gets up, the seed sprouts and grows, though he does not know how. All by itself the soil produces grain— first the stalk, then the head, then the full kernel in the head. As soon as the grain is ripe, he puts the sickle to it, because the harvest has come.

MARK 4:27

money as seed. When you make this paradigm shift in how you view money, y[ou] will deal with your personal finances much differently.

Redeemed from the curse

When you apply faith in God to your seed, it will produce results. God wants [to] reward and bless us. The original curse, which came upon all of us through t[he] disobedience of Adam and Eve, still operates on individuals who don't live throu[gh] Christ. However, Christ redeemed us from that curse by becoming a curse for [us] (Galatians 3:13) When we come to Christ this curse does not have any right [to] operate in us. It is a personal choice—whether to trust in God or in circumstanc[e]. Both God and circumstance are real in your life. But you will have to make t[he] decision who you partner with: God or circumstances. Your will is the director [of] your life. Choose the right partner in order to become an overcomer.

The difference between seeds and tithes

We bring our tithes to God after we've received an income. We sow seeds in ord[er] to receive an income. Tithes belongs to God. Tithes are thanksgiving and al[so] seed. We sow seeds in order to receive a harvest; sowing is done on purpose.

Seeds come first and produce a harvest. Tithes are paid from the harvest. It [is] an ongoing process. The Creator puts it in motion and it will work in every area [of] your life, and for everyone under the sun.

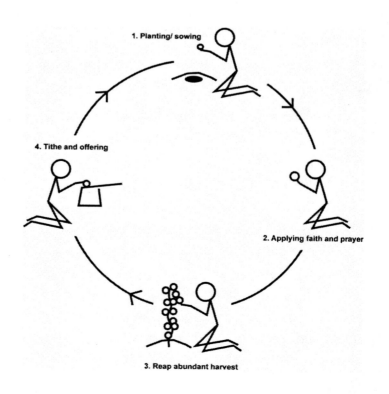

1. Planting/ sowing

2. Applying faith and prayer

3. Reap abundant harvest

4. Tithe and offering

Review today's lesson.

1. Prayerfully choose one statement or verse that was most meaningful to you today.

_____

_____

_____

2. Write a prayer of response.

_____

_____

_____

_____

_____

_____

3. What action do you need to take in response to today's lesson?

_____

_____

_____

_____

_____

POWER POINTS

- Without faith it is impossible to please God.
- Faith gives you the edge in the system of seedtime and harvest.
- Your seed can produce an abundant harvest when it is charged with faith in God.
- Christ redeemed us from the original curse by becoming a curse for us.
- Your seed is anything that helps another person.
- Seedtime and harvest operates regardless of your personal belief system.

Day 3

Journal

TITHES

Tithes are God's idea.

- Tithes were introduced by God, established by His Word and executed by the Holy Spirit. (Leviticus 27:30-34)
- Tithes started before the Old Testament laws (Genesis 14:18-20)
- Tithes teach us to fear the Lord (Deuteronomy 14:22-23)

Reflect on Deuteronomy 26:1-3

And it shall be, when you come into the land which the LORD your God is giving you as an inheritance, and you possess it and dwell in it, that you shall take some of the first of all the produce of the ground, which you shall bring from your land that the LORD your God is giving you, and put it in a basket and go to the place where the LORD your God chooses to make His name abide.

In your own words, what are tithes?

_____

_____

_____

Honor the Lord with thy substance, and with the first fruits of all your income; so shall your storage places be filled with plenty, and your vats be overflowing with new wine.

PROVERBS 3:9-10

Who do we present our tithes to?

Hebrews 7:1-6

For this Melchizedek, king of Salem, priest of the Most High God, who met Abraham returning from the slaughter of the kings and blessed him, to whom also Abraham gave a tenth part of all, first being translated "king of righteousness," and then also king of Salem, meaning "king of peace," without father, without mother, without genealogy, having neither beginning of days nor end of life, but made like the Son of God, remains a priest continually. Now consider how great this man was, to whom even the patriarch Abraham gave a tenth of the spoils. And indeed those who are of the sons of Levi, who receive the priesthood, have a commandment to receive tithes from the people according to the law, that is, from their brethren, though they have come from the loins

of Abraham; but he whose genealogy is not derived from them received tithes from Abraham and blessed him who had the promises.

To whom did Abraham give his tithe?

_____

_____

_____

What was the purpose behind Abraham's action?

_____

_____

_____

Abraham brought tithes to Melchizedek, the high priest. We don't know his beginning—all we know is that he was the king of Salem. Abraham's action was simple obedience. His heart recognized God's authority. For us, Jesus is our High Priest and we present our offerings to Jesus, who in turn present our offerings to the Father. We should maintain the heart of Abraham, not the heart of Cain. Obedience is better than sacrifice.

Hebrews 3:1

Therefore, holy brethren, partakers of the heavenly calling, consider the Apostle and High Priest of our confession, Christ Jesus.

According to Hebrews 3:1 who is our High Priest?

_____

_____

_____

Malachi 3:8-10 (NIV)

Will a man rob God? Yet you rob me. But you ask, "How do we rob you?"In tithes and offerings. You are under a curse—the whole nation of you—because you are robbing me. Bring the whole tithe into the storehouse, that there may be food in my house. Test me in this, says the Lord Almighty, and see if I will not throw open the floodgates of heaven and pour out so much blessing that you will not have room enough for it.

What is the purpose of tithes?

_____

_____

_____

To tithe is really to give back to God from the harvest He has blessed you with. Tithes are the substance—the tangible substance—and the fruits of your labour, usually money. It is not a man-made idea to tithe; God commanded the Israelites to bring the firstfruits of their labour to Him. Even before that, in Genesis 14:20, Abram gave Melchizedek the priest a tenth of what God had blessed him with as part of the spoils of war. The purpose of tithing is to fill God's storehouse—His church.

Why do we tithe?

- Tithes initiate wisdom. (Proverbs 22:4)
- Tithes protect our job, our fields and our material possessions. (Malachi 3:11; Proverbs 3:9-10)
- Tithes multiply our blessings by protecting our jobs. (Malachi 3:10)
- Tithes protect our health. (Malachi 3:11)
- Tithes bring favour in the sight of God and man. (2 Corinthians 9:8)
- Tithes build our eternal rewards. (2 Corinthians 9:10)

Tithing is confessing God's promises by faith

Many of us don't pay attention when we bring our tithes to the Lord. We quickly drop the envelope in the basket and don't spend too much time thinking about it. Tithing, as God originally intended it, constitutes the actual words we say that accompany our action of bringing the tithe. It should not be taken lightly. When we bring our tithes, it really is an act of worship, representing the fruit of our lives. We present our tithes to Jesus, our Most High Priest, who in turn will set it before the altar of God. Tithing is the process by which we bring our tithes to God.

Deuteronomy 26:2-3

That you shall take some of the first of all the produce of the ground, which you shall bring from your land that the LORD your God is giving you, and put it in a basket and go to the place where the LORD your God chooses to make His name abide. And you shall go to the one who is priest in those days, and say to him, `I declare today to the LORD your God that I have come to the country which the LORD swore to our fathers to give us. Then the priest shall take the basket out of your hand and set it down before the altar of the LORD your God.

Tithing is done with the mouth. Deuteronomy 26:13-15 is an example of what we can say as we bring our tithe to God:

I have removed from my house the sacred portion and have given it to the Levite, the alien, the fatherless and the widow, according to all you commanded. I have not turned

aside from your commands nor have I forgotten any of them. I have not eaten any of the sacred portion while I was in mourning, nor have I removed any of it while I was unclean, nor have I offered any of it to the dead. I have obeyed the Lord my God; I have done everything you commanded me. Look down from heaven, your holy dwelling place, and bless your people Israel and the land you have given us as you promised on oath to our forefathers, a land flowing with milk and honey.

Now write down your own tithing statement to say next time you bring your tithe to God.

_____

_____

_____

_____

_____

_____

_____

_____

_____

_____

_____

_____

_____

_____

Tithing should be done intentionally, in an attitude of praise and thanksgiving, and covered with prayer. We pray in the expectation that God will reward our obedience and watch to see how God responds. Just like a farmer anticipates that his seeds will grow, we anticipate God's activity in direct answer to our prayer and obedience.

A practical suggestion:

Once I discovered the importance of both tithes and tithing, I faced the challenge of giving my tithe and praying over it. I decided to start a tithe account in the bank. Now as soon as I get my paycheck, I remove my tithe into the tithe account. By doing so, I know exactly how much I have and I also regularly take time during my devotions to pray over the tithe. I meditate and ask the Spirit where I should give and how much. I have been maintaining this tithe account for the last 20 years and have experienced God's blessing, increase and protection.

Review today's lesson.

1. Prayerfully choose one statement or verse that was most meaningful to you today.

_____

_____

_____

2. Write a prayer of response.

_____

_____

_____

_____

_____

_____

_____

_____

_____

_____

3. What action do you need to take in response to today's lesson?

_____

_____

_____

POWER POINTS

- Tithes are God's idea.
- To tithe is to give back to God from the harvest He blessed you with.
- Tithes are the tangible substance of your labour.
- The purpose of tithes is to fill the storehouse of God.
- Tithing is the process by which we bring our tithes to God.
- Tithing is an act of worship, presenting the fruit of our lives to Jesus.

Journal

GIVING

The Merriam-Webster Dictionary states that to give is, "to make a present of; to bestow by formal action; to accord or yield to another ... to put into the possession or keeping of another."

Define giving in your own words.

_____

_____

_____

Why do you think giving is important?

_____

_____

_____

_____

Giving is like planting seeds in the spirit realm. You must plant in order to harvest; you must give in order to receive.

Giving to God: a joyful deposit into the Kingdom system

Colossians 1:12-13 says, "... (give) thanks to the Father, who has qualified you to share in the inheritance of the saints in the kingdom of light. For he has rescued us from the dominion of darkness and brought us into the kingdom of the Son he loves, in whom we have redemption, the forgiveness of sins."

Through Jesus' blood we are saved by grace. He redeemed us from the original curse. He took us out of darkness and planted us in the Kingdom of light. By our faith in the finished work of Christ we are entitled to live in the Kingdom of God and obtain our inheritance. God has provided for us a way by which we can live successfully on this earth. We can build our eternal

> Give, and it will be given to you: good measure, pressed down, shaken together, and running over will be put into your bosom. For with the same measure that you use, it will be measured back to you.
>
> LUKE 6:38

inheritance through our material possessions and invest it where rust and moth will not corrupt it. We invest into the Kingdom of God when we give—of ourselves, our time, and our material possessions. It is not about how much we have to give, but how we give. Jesus illustrated this clearly when he pointed out the example of the widow and her offering.

Please read Mark 12:41-44. What made the widow's offering different from every other offering at the temple that day?

_____

_____

_____

God always looks at the attitude of our heart; also in giving. Cain and Able brought the fruit of their work to God as offerings. Genesis 4:2-5 (NIV) says, "Now Abel kept flocks, and Cain worked the soil. In the course of time Cain brought some of the fruits of the soil as an offering to the Lord. But Abel brought fat portions from some of the firstborn of his flock. The Lord looked with favor on Abel and his offering, but on Cain and his offering he did not look with favor."

Why do you think God rejected Cain's offering? In the beginning, God taught them to bring their offerings to Him. It consisted of the sacrifice of an animal—the way God decided to deal with the problem of sin. At that time God had not introduced any other kind of offering. The issue was obedience, recognizing God as the Author and Director of our lives. Cain could easily have exchanged his grains for an animal with his brother.

Our giving exposes the sin in our lives. Cain's heart was not right towards his brother and neither was it right towards God. Cain wanted to respect God in his own way. But God wanted to point out the seed of jealousy in Cain's heart and wanted him to rule over this sin. Cain eventually committed the first murder in the history of mankind. If Cain had asked God to bring him into understanding, God could have explained to him his faults and history might have been different.

Read 2 Corinthians 9:6-11 and answer the questions that follow.

How should we give?

_____

_____

_____

What kind of giver would you like to be? .

_____

_____

_____

(If you like, ask God right now to help you.)

According to verse 11, what is the purpose for being blessed?

_____

_____

_____

Giving out of our need

In 1972 we decided to leave India and move to the United States. Our motivation was birthed from meditation on the Word of God. My husband did his Masters Degree in Forestry at LSU and through a series of supernaturally guided incidents we ended up in Canada. We immediately faced severe financial challenges and went through some very difficult times. Our struggles did not come in the areas of health or relationships, but rather in our finances.

When we left India, we did not do so in the hope of a better economic situation. Our sincere desire was to live a life that was pleasing to God and truthful before Him.

After my husband finished his degree in Forestry he had difficulty finding a job in his field of expertise. It was right after we had moved to Canada, we were new immigrants and we felt very lonely and quite discouraged. There was nobody we could turn to for help. We had no relatives, friends or even acquaintances in Canada and we couldn't find proper jobs. Although we were attending a church where people knew we needed suitable jobs, for over two and half years no one offered to help us.

As finances became even more difficult for us, the first thing we did, was to stop tithing. I believe that was the biggest mistake we ever made. By His grace, however, and through this experience, God taught us the importance of tithing. He showed us how tithing was directly connected to our financial well-being and increase in life. We cried on each others' shoulders and cried out to God. As we persisted in looking to God for help, we prayed intently and also fasted.

In 1969, while still in India, I read a book called _Seed Faith_ by Oral Roberts. The Holy Spirit brought the contents of that book to my memory and I went back to compare it with the Scriptures. I did a word-search in my Bible about

seeds and tithing and I realized that I ought to start planting some seeds. I decided to start from scratch and plant some seeds.

I had virtually nothing to give to God. Since the Indian Government at that time allowed me to bring only $20 in foreign currency, we came to North America with two suitcases of clothes. But I did have some gold jewelry and so I decided to plant these as seeds. I called my pastor and gave all the jewelry to be sold and used as offering. I did what I found in the Word of God to start this journey with Him into the financial realm.

Our financial situation did not change overnight. But our thinking and our attitudes started to change. God also started guiding us in new and different directions. We moved to a new church where someone helped my husband find a job as an assistant bank manager, while I got involved in Real Estate. Soon after, our financial situation changed drastically.

As we got ahold of God's principles and gave according to God's Word, leading a life acceptable to God, we prospered. My income in Real Estate started to double every year for eight years in a row. We bought our first home and God blessed us with two sons. A while later we moved into our dream home, and we could even send our sons to a private school. We were truly blessed and I learned that God's Word is true.

God's ways are higher then our ways and His thoughts are higher than our thoughts.

Reflect on the following verses:

2 Samuel 22:31
As for God, His way is perfect; the word of the LORD is proven; he is a shield to all who trust in Him.

_____

_____

Isaiah 55:8
For My thoughts are not your thoughts, nor are your ways My ways, says the LORD.

_____

_____

You are very different from your spouse or even your next-door neighbour. We all tend to try and fit into the mould of a "successful" person. We cannot be successful by following somebody else's example. We have to make the garment fit us. God is the only One who knows us. Even we do not understand ourselves as well as He does.

Trusting God will unlock many keys to your life. There is no negotiation with God. He has designed you and you live in an earthly suit, called your body. You will only become a winner by partnering with Him. He does not want to control you, but He wants to give you the best.

Proverbs 3:12-16

For whom the LORD loves He corrects, just as a father the son in whom he delights. Happy is the man who finds wisdom, and the man who gains understanding; For her proceeds are better than the profits of silver, and her gain than fine gold. She is more precious than rubies, and all the things you may desire cannot compare with her. Length of days is in her right hand, in her left hand riches and honor.

Psalm 112:1-3

Praise the LORD! Blessed is the man who fears the LORD, who delights greatly in His commandments. His descendants will be mighty on earth; the generation of the upright will be blessed. Wealth and riches will be in his house, and his righteousness endures forever.

Review today's lesson.

1. Prayerfully choose one statement or verse that was most meaningful to you today.

_____

_____

_____

_____

2. Write a prayer of response.

_____

_____

_____

_____

_____

_____

_____

_____

_____

3. What action do you need to take in response to today's lesson?

_____

_____

_____

_____

_____

_____

_____

_____

POWER POINTS

- Giving is like planting seeds in the spirit realm.
- You have to give in order to receive.
- You can build your eternal inheritance through your material possessions by investing it where rust and moth will not corrupt it.
- God does not want to control you, He wants to give you His best.

Journal

ESSION V

GOD'S SYSTEM OF GUIDANCE

HIS WORD

For Ezra had devoted himself to the study and observance of the Law of the Lord, and to teaching its decrees and laws in Israel.

EZRA 7:10 (NIV)

God's Word contains all the knowledge we may need to be successful. The Holy Spirit is our personal counselor, who highlights the perfect Scriptures at appropriate times, guiding us into revelation knowledge and a very personal and unique relationship with God, our Master Financier.

God's Word is living and active. When we apply it, His Word brings life. You can build your life on the foundation of His Word.

It is vitally important to be single-minded in God's Word. James 1:8 says, "(H)e who doubts is like a wave of the sea driven and tossed by the wind. For let not that man suppose that he will receive anything from the Lord; he is a double-minded man, unstable in all his ways."

Since we are spirit, have a soul, and live in a body, outward change is usually temporary; our spirit, which is the inner man, has to change first for any true transformation to take place. This can only happen as we commune with God and meditate on His Word regularly. But once we get to the place where we trust the words flowing from the mouth of God and take meaningful steps in response, we will experience new freedom in our finances.

God gave us specific instructions in His Word on how we can enter into our Promised Land. It is not impossible to attain, but requires our diligent searching of His Word and then trusting His Word. God is the same yesterday, today and tomorrow. What God showed the Israelites, Jesus taught His disciples and we too can follow His careful instructions.

Proverbs 16:20 (NIV) says, "Whoever gives heed to instruction prospers, and blessed is he who trusts in the Lord."

In my early days of desperately searching the Word of God, two passages of Scripture impacted me tremendously.

The first was 3 John 2 (KJV): "Beloved, I wish above all things that thou mayest prosper and be in health, even as thy soul prospereth."

But the verse that probably impacted me most, was Joshua 1:8-9 "This Book of the Law shall not depart from your mouth, but you shall meditate in it day and night, For then you will make your way prosperous, and then you

will have good success."

To me, these words are paralleled by Jesus' instruction in Matthew 6:33 (KJV), "But seek ye first the kingdom of God, and his righteousness, and all these things shall be added unto you."

I realized that Joshua 1:8-9 contained certain steps. I divided it into four steps and tested them:

Step one: This Book of the Law shall not depart from your mouth

Step two: But you shall meditate on it day and night

Step three: For then you will make your way prosperous

Step four: and then you will have good success

When we first arrived in this country, as new immigrants, we needed an enormous amount of help. My husband and I had neither family nor friends in North America. During the difficult time of not finding good work we questioned our faith, but I had nobody to turn to except God. In turn, the Holy Spirit pointed me to the Word of God and helped me to apply what I was learning. We were willing to go any length to live according to His Word. I was convinced that whatever is written in the Bible, if I applied it, it would work. I decided to test it by taking action.

I used four by six recipe cards and wrote down Joshua 1:8. I replaced "your" with "my" and "you" with "I." I posted these around my home in

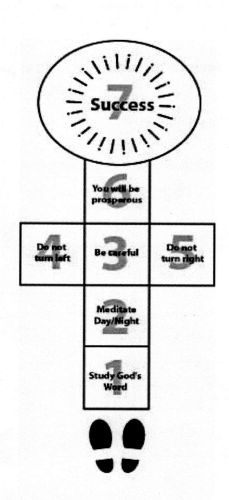

Joshua 1:8-9 Steps

strategic places where I could see them daily. I also carried one in my purse. I took time to think on it and pray about it all day long. I still communed with God early in the morning, but I meditated on these words all day, without having to stop working.

Things started changing inside me. Confidence, boldness and faith started to replace fear, and hope entered my heart. Combined with faith, and the leading of the Holy Spirit, God opened up the Scriptures to me and led me step by step into new faith adventures.

Again, let's reflect on Joshua 1:6-9 (NIV).

Be strong and courageous, because you will lead these people to inherit the land I swore to their forefathers to give them. Be strong and very courageous. Be careful to obey all the law my servant Moses gave you; do not turn from it to the right or to the left, that you may be successful wherever you go. Do not let this Book of the Law depart from your mouth; meditate on it day and night, so that you may be careful to do everything written in it. Then you will be prosperous and successful. Have I not commanded you? Be strong and courageous. Do not be terrified; do not be discouraged, for the Lord your God will be with you wherever you go.

Now reword the above Scripture passage and make it personal:

For example: I will not let this Book of the Law depart from my mouth.

___ will meditate on it day and night, so that ___ may be careful to do everything written in it. Then ___ will be prosperous and successful. Have I not commanded you? Be strong and courageous. Do not be terrified, do not be discouraged, for the Lord ___ God will be with ___ wherever ___ go.

_____

_____

_____

_____

_____

_____

_____

_____

_____

_____

_____

God's Word is established in the spiritual realm to bring us results in the physical world. It is our relationship with God and knowledge about the Word of God which determines the outcome. Our life is not hidden from God but is hidden from others. They can see God working in our life through the results manifested in our marriage, family life, job, and finances. People often judge us based on our financial state. While this may not be fair and does not make life any easier, society tends to judge us according to our financial capacity.

Review today's lesson.

1. Prayerfully choose one statement or verse that was most meaningful to you today.

_____

_____

_____

2. Write a prayer of response.

_____

_____

_____

_____

_____

_____

_____

_____

_____

3. What action do you need to take in response to today's lesson?

_____

_____

_____

_____

POWER POINTS

- You are a spirit, you have a soul, and you live in a body.
- God's Word is established in the spiritual realm to bring you results in the physical world.
- Meditate on God's Word day and night.
- God's Word guides us into all Truth.

Day 1

Journal

THE HOLY SPIRIT IS YOUR PERSONAL GUIDE

Your intimate relationship with God in prayer, meditation, and study of the Bible will be an integral and indispensable part of the results you will see. John 14:26 reminds us that the Holy Spirit is our personal teacher. The Holy Spirit will guide you into all truth as you apply God's Word to every circumstance. Our financial situations are all very different and we need Him as our personal consultant to know how to deal with our unique circumstances.

God reveals His intention for our life on earth through Scripture. From Genesis through Revelation He has demonstrated His work in the lives of His people. We all have to come to a place where we know God is more than willing to intervene in our situations and help direct our lives. We have to come to a place of trust, where we believe that His plans for us are always good and compassionate.

> But the Counselor, the Holy Spirit, whom the Father will send in my name, will teach you all things and will remind you of everything I have said to you.
>
> JOHN 14:26 (NIV)

How does God meet the needs of His people?

Consider the following three examples from the Bible where God showed up in the midst of overwhelming material need.

2 Kings 4:1-10

A certain woman of the wives of the sons of the prophets cried out to Elisha, saying, "Your servant my husband is dead, and you know that your servant feared the LORD. And the creditor is coming to take my two sons to be his slaves." So Elisha said to her, 'What shall I do for you? Tell me, what do you have in the house?' And she said, "Your maidservant has nothing in the house but a jar of oil." Then he said, "Go, borrow vessels from everywhere, from all your neighbors empty vessels; do not gather just a few.

Day 2

And when you have come in, you shall shut the door behind you and your sons; then pour it into all those vessels, and set aside the full ones." So she went from him and shut the door behind her and her sons, who brought the vessels to her; and she poured it out. Now it came to pass, when the vessels were full, that she said to her son, "Bring me another vessel." And he said to her, "There is not another vessel." So the oil ceased. Then she came and told the man of God. And he said, "Go, sell the oil and pay your debt; and you and your sons live on the rest."

How did God meet this widow's need?

_____

_____

_____

_____

_____

1 Kings 17:1-6

And Elijah the Tishbite, of the inhabitants of Gilead, said to Ahab, "As the LORD God of Israel lives, before whom I stand, there shall not be dew nor rain these years, except at my word." Then the word of the LORD came to him, saying, "Get away from here and turn eastward, and hide by the Brook Cherith, which flows into the Jordan. And it will be that you shall drink from the brook, and I have commanded the ravens to feed you there." So he went and did according to the word of the LORD, for he went and stayed by the Brook Cherith, which flows into the Jordan. The ravens brought him bread and meat in the morning, and bread and meat in the evening; and he drank from the brook.

How did God meet Elijah's need?

_____

_____

_____

_____

_____

1 Kings 17:8-15

Then the word of the LORD came to him, saying, "Arise, go to Zarephath, which belongs to Sidon, and dwell there. See, I have commanded a widow there to provide for you." So he arose and went to Zarephath. And when he came to the gate of the city, indeed a widow was there gathering sticks. And he called to her and said, "Please bring

me a little water in a cup, that I may drink." And as she was going to get it, he called to her and said, "Please bring me a morsel of bread in your hand." So she said, "As the LORD your God lives, I do not have bread, only a handful of flour in a bin, and a little oil in a jar; and see, I am gathering a couple of sticks that I may go in and prepare it for myself and my son, that we may eat it, and die." And Elijah said to her, "Do not fear; go and do as you have said, but make me a small cake from it first, and bring it to me; and afterward make some for yourself and your son. For thus says the LORD God of Israel: 'The bin of flour shall not be used up, nor shall the jar of oil run dry, until the day the LORD sends rain on the earth.'" So she went away and did according to the word of Elijah; and she and he and her household ate for many days.

How did God meet His servants' need in this case?

_____

_____

_____

God is always at work, thinking about you. What needs do you have right now?

_____

_____

_____

Based on the above three stories, write a statement of belief about what God can do for you to meet your needs.

_____

_____

_____

_____

_____

_____

_____

Emotions and the Word of God

Our unregenerate emotion can cause great harm. Never consider the Word of God from a purely emotional point of view. God's Word stands alone.

Emotion expresses the mind of the flesh. Choosing to follow God's Word with our spirit and surrendered will, makes our mind unfruitful and our

Day 2

emotions meaningless. Faith in God's Word is an action of our will. After we've made the choice to live according to His Word, God again uses our mind and emotions, because God has a purpose for every part of our faculties.

Hebrews 4:12-13

For the Word of God is living and powerful, sharper than any two-edged sword, piercing even to the division of soul and spirit and of joints and marrow and is a discerner of the thoughts and intents of the heart. And there is no creature hidden from his sight, but all things are naked and open to the eyes of Him to whom we must give account.

1 Peter 1:13

Therefore gird up the loins of your mind, be sober, and rest your hope fully upon the grace that is to be brought to you at the revelation of Jesus Christ.

A self-centered heart responds to God's Word in an emotional way. Human reasoning will not give you God's perspective. God takes the initiative to show us His purpose and plan through His Word. He speaks to us in our quiet times with Him. He wants to bless us and give us the desires of our heart. But He may want us to adjust our present life and believe wholly in His Word. A study of God's Word will show that God leaves people right where they're at, unless they learn to change and go with Him.

God's written Word is His instruction for our lives. Until we learn to listen and trust His Word, He may leave us right where we are. But the moment we obey and adjust our financial situation according to His revealed Word, we will come to experience His abundant grace.

Review today's lesson.

1. Prayerfully choose one statement or verse that was most meaningful to you today.

_____

_____

_____

2. Write a prayer of response.

_____

_____

_____

_____

_____

_____

_____

_____

_____

_____

_____

3. What action do you need to take in response to today's lesson?

_____

_____

_____

POWER POINTS

- The Holy Spirit is your personal teacher.
- The Holy Spirit is your God-appointed Counselor.
- The Holy Spirit will guide you into all truth.
- The Holy Spirit will bring revelation to God's Word.
- Refrain from considering the Word of God from a purely emotional perspective.
- Faith in the Word of God is an act of will.
- When you obey God according to His revealed Word, you will come to experience His abundant grace.

Journal

Day 2

GOD GRANTS UNIQUE OPPORTUNITIES

God grabs our attention through His Word

While reading the Scripture and meditating, the Holy Spirit often directs my attention to a passage in the Bible or a life story of a person that lines up with the Word of God. I pay very careful attention to those words. I write them down, meditate on them and adjust my life accordingly.

God will not show you your next move until you've adjusted yourself to the first move according to His revelation. I purposely alert myself to listen to my spirit. If there is any disobedience or sin I am aware of in my life, I repent. My commitment to changing my life determines the working of the Word in my situation and circumstances.

Reflect on the following passage of Scripture:

Psalm 1:1-6

Blessed is the man who walks not in the counsel of the ungodly, nor stands in the path of sinners, nor sits in the seat of the scornful; but his delight is in the law of the LORD, and in His law he meditates day and night. He shall be like a tree planted by the rivers of water, that brings forth its fruit in its season, whose leaf also shall not wither; and whatever he does shall prosper. The ungodly are not so, but are like the chaff which the wind drives away. Therefore the ungodly shall not stand in the judgment, nor sinners in the congregation of the righteous. For the LORD knows the way of the righteous, but the way of the ungodly shall perish.

I call heaven and earth as witnesses today against you, that I have set before you life and death, blessing and cursing; therefore choose life, that both you and your descendants may live.

DEUTERONOMY 30:19

_____

_____

_____

_____

_____

_____

God deals uniquely with each individual in similar circumstances.

When God called Abram out of his country, He instructed him to go to Egy
and stay there because there was a great famine in the land and it would last f
a few years.

Genesis 12:10

Now there was a famine in the land, and Abram went down to Egypt to dwell there,
the famine was severe in the land

God is able to protect a person in the midst of famine. God chose to ser
Abram to live in Egypt during that time. After the famine was over, Abra
returned to the original place where God had instructed him to live.

After many years, the famine occurred again in the same place. Now Isa
faced the same situation and he had to make decisions concerning his family ar
livestock. He was very rich and was responsible for all his household. So h
decided to make a smart move.

Genesis 26:1-2

There was a famine in the land, besides the first famine that was in the days of Abrahan
And Isaac went to Abimelech king of the Philistines, in Gerar. Then the LORD appear
to him and said: "Do not go down to Egypt; live in the land of which I shall tell you."

Genesis 26:12-13

Then Isaac sowed in that land, and reaped in the same year a hundredfold; and the LOR
blessed him. The man began to prosper, and continued prospering until he became ve
prosperous.

When you read the whole chapter you will find out that God blessed Isaac i
the midst of famine. He became a living testimony of God's provision. All the kin
feared and respected him. Isaac could have earned that respect and attention b
his own ability, but God gave it to Him instead, since he was obedient. His way
are truly higher then our ways. His thoughts are always good towards us.

When we ask God for guidance, we cannot copy anybody; instead we need to stay connected to God by meditating on His Word, praying and associating with godly people.

As I discovered the power of the Word of God in my life, I faced a personal challenge. Merely two years into my Real Estate career, the economic situation in our country took a downturn. Interest rates rose at a rapid rate to 22 percent. It became very difficult to sell real estate. Since it was our main source of income, I went to the Lord and His Word. That passage where God provided for Abraham and Isaac during a time of famine, rooted my faith. During that hard economic time, God provided for us through Real Estate and we didn't lack anything. I did business as usual and I still had clients who wanted to buy and sell.

The Holy Spirit led me to make some changes in my life and stay focused on God's Word, rather than the destructive news about the economic climate, and so to prevent fear from entering my life. Although I had to know what was going on in the world, in order to make reasonable decisions, I had to purpose not to focus on the "gloom and doom" news. I had to draw a fine line between being informed and putting my hope and trust in the economic system. I still apply this valuable principle in my life today.

In 1985 my business was booming. But in the midst of that prosperous time I heard in my heart God's prompting for our family to move to British Columbia. I didn't know much about the province, but the impression in my heart was so strong that I consulted with family and friends. I valued their opinion more than the guidance of the Holy Spirit and we didn't move. The Real Estate market collapsed and we lost everything. Eight years later we ended up in B.C. My disobedience to God's guidance cost us dearly. But definitely the highest price for my disobedience was God's silence. Although I prayed, fasted and cried out to God, He remained silent.

Why do you think God dealt differently with Abraham and Isaac under similar situations?

_____

_____

_____

What is the key to success revealed in these life stories?

_____

_____

_____

The key is to be in the perfect will of God. We should never challenge God on His words and His instructions. God wants to give us more than what we can imagine or even think.

Reflect on the following Scriptures:

Ephesians 3:20-21

Now to Him who is able to do exceedingly abundantly above all that we ask or think, according to the power that works in us, to Him be glory in the church by Christ Jesus to all generations, forever and ever. Amen.

_____

_____

_____

1 Corinthians 2:10-12

But God has revealed them to us through His Spirit. For the Spirit searches all things, yes, the deep things of God. For what man knows the things of a man except the spirit of the man which is in him? Even so no one knows the things of God except the Spirit of God. Now we have received, not the spirit of the world, but the Spirit who is from God, that we might know the things that have been freely given to us by God.

_____

_____

_____

Responding to God's silence

Whenever it feels like God is silent in your life, you can respond in one of the following ways: First, check your sin list and your disobedience list. If there is none, then wait on the Lord. Perhaps He is preparing you to go into a deeper understanding. He wants you to move up to a level where He can entrust you with higher work.

During a time of uncertainty, you can only be positive if you know your Provider intimately, because you know there is no fear in perfect love.

In my own life, I had to develop this trust by first being completely devoted to God and His Word. The moment I realized His love for me and my family, my fear of the future disappeared. I had to make a major attitude adjustment toward Him and His Word so that I could expect from Him in faith and trust.

I also had to learn to understand our enemy who continuously tries to undermine us. It will be foolishness on our part if we do not consider the works of the enemy and be prepared to face him boldly. We should not run from him—rather he must run from us. We don't have to pray repeatedly in order to make God listen to us but we pray persistently to gain freedom from the kingdom of darkness. We enforce the redeemed work of Christ in the enemy's land.

Daniel 9:20-23

Now while I was speaking, praying, and confessing my sin and the sin of my people Israel, and presenting my supplication before the LORD my God for the holy mountain of my God, yes, while I was speaking in prayer, the man Gabriel, whom I had seen in the vision at the beginning, being caused to fly swiftly, reached me about the time of the evening offering. And he informed me, and talked with me, and said, "O Daniel, I have now come forth to give you skill to understand. At the beginning of your supplications the command went out, and I have come to tell you, for you are greatly beloved; therefore consider the matter, and understand the vision..."

_____

_____

_____

Daniel 10:12 -13

Then he said to me, "Do not fear, Daniel, for from the first day that you set your heart to understand, and to humble yourself before your God, your words were heard; and I have come because of your words. But the prince of the kingdom of Persia withstood me twenty-one days; and behold, Michael, one of the chief princes, came to help me, for I had been left alone there with the kings of Persia."

_____

_____

_____

Ephesians 6:10-12

Finally, my brethren, be strong in the Lord and in the power of His might. Put on the whole armor of God, that you may be able to stand against the wiles of the devil. For we do not wrestle against flesh and blood, but against principalities, against powers, against the rulers of the darkness of this age, against spiritual hosts of wickedness in the heavenly places.

If you have sown your seed, paid your tithes, heard the Word from God, and done according to His Word then continue to do the last thing that God

Day 3

told you to do and watch and wait for a fresh revelation about your financial matters. God holds your future in His hands. Your trust in Him will unlock your abundant life now. Paul said, "If you are willing and obedient you will eat the good of the land."

Review today's lesson.

1. Prayerfully choose one statement or verse that was most meaningful to you today.

_____

_____

_____

2. Write a prayer of response.

_____

_____

_____

_____

_____

_____

_____

_____

_____

_____

_____

_____

_____

_____

_____

3. What action do you need to take in response to today's lesson?

_____

_____

_____

_____

_____

_____

POWER POINTS

- God will not reveal your next step until you've adjusted to the first move according to His revelation.
- Your commitment to change determines the work of the Word in your life.
- God always guides you uniquely.
- You can't copy God's guidance to anyone else.
- Respond to God's silence by first checking your sin.
- God holds your future in His hands.
- Trusting God will unlock your abundant life.

Journal

GOD'S COVENANT

Read Deuteronomy 7:12-15

Then it shall come to pass, because you listen to these judgments, and keep and do them, that the Lord your God will keep with you the covenant and the mercy which He swore to your fathers. And He will love you and bless you and multiply you; He will also bless the fruit of your womb and the fruit of your land, your grain and your new wine and your oil, the increase of your cattle and the offspring of your flock, in the land of which He swore to your fathers to give you. You shall be blessed above all peoples; there shall not be a male or female barren among you or your livestock. And the Lord will take away from you all sickness.

God's covenant contains both His word and His promises. God made certain promises and gave His word that it would happen.

God's Word contains His facts and His promises.

Facts and Promises

God's facts have to be appropriated, while His promises have to be obeyed. Promises can be conditional or unconditional. With the Old Covenant, God gave us laws that needed to be obeyed.

Reflect on Galatians 3:19-25

What purpose then does the law serve? It was added because of transgressions, till the Seed should come to whom the promise was made; and it was appointed through angels by the hand of a mediator. Now a mediator does not mediate for one only, but God is one. Is the law then against the promises of God? Certainly not! For if there had been a law given which could have given life, truly righteousness would have been the law. But the Scripture has confined all under sin, that the promise of faith in Jesus Christ might be given to those who believe. But before faith came, we were kept under guard by the law, kept for the faith which would afterward be revealed. Therefore the law was our tutor to bring us to Christ, that we might be justified by faith. But after faith has come, we are no longer under a tutor.

Therefore know that the Lord your God, He is God, the faithful God who keeps covenant and mercy for a thousand generations with those who love Him and keep His commandments.

DEUTERONOMY 7:9-10

In your own words, what is the purpose of the Law?

_____

_____

_____

_____

The Old Covenant pointed to our inability and total dependence on God. God promised blessings, but these were conditional to our obedience.

Read Deuteronomy 28:2-65

What were the results of disobedience? What is the impact on the human race?

_____

_____

_____

Deuteronomy 28:2-14 explain the blessings, while verses 15-68 describe the curses.

When the curse came in with sin, it covered our spirit, soul and body. These curses contained our eternal damnation, continued lack and sickness.

When Christ came and redeemed us from the curse of the Law, He redeemed us from all the consequences of the curse—eternal damnation, lack and sickness. But our redemption is not automatic.

Reflect on Galatians 3:13-14 and then answer the following questions:

In your opinion, what does the curse of the law as described in Galatians 3:13 mean?

_____

_____

What does it mean to you personally, that Christ became "the curse for us?"

_____

_____

_____

God originally established His covenant with Abraham in Genesis 12:1-3. This covenant was fulfilled through Jesus Christ who established the new covenant by becoming a curse for us. This means that now anyone can enter into this same covenant through faith in Jesus Christ. If we walk in God's commandments, we no longer have to suffer the consequences of sin under which the world's system operates.

Deuteronomy 30:11-14

For this commandment which I command you today, it is not too mysterious for you, nor is it far off. It is not in heaven, that you should say, "Who will ascend into heaven for us and bring it to us, that we may hear it and do it?" Nor is it beyond the sea, that you should say, "Who will go over the sea for us and bring it to us; that we may hear it and do it? But the word is very near you, in your mouth and in your heart, that you may do it.

Because of Christ, the above Scripture has been fulfilled, and became God's fact. Now it is up to us to appropriate it and live in it.

Reflect on the above Scripture and ask God to show you what you must do to live successfully according to His Word?

_____
_____
_____
_____
_____

Read Deuteronomy 30:19-20 (NIV)

This day I call heaven and earth as witnesses against you that I have set before you life and death, blessings and curses. Now choose life, so that you and your children may live and that you may love the Lord your God, listen to his voice, and hold fast to him. For the Lord is your life.

What do you choose today? Life or death?

_____
_____
_____
_____

Blessings or curses?

_____

_____

_____

Review today's lesson.

1. Prayerfully choose one statement or verse that was most meaningful to you today.

_____

_____

_____

2. Write a prayer of response.

_____

_____

_____

_____

_____

_____

_____

3. What action do you need to take in response to today's lesson?

_____

_____

_____

POWER POINTS

- God's facts have to be appropriated.
- God's promises have to be obeyed.
- The Old Covenant pointed to our inability and total dependence on God.
- When Christ redeemed us from the curse of the Law, He redeemed us from all the consequences of the curse—eternal damnation, lack and sickness.

*J*ournal

SESSION 5
Day 4

God's Covenant Promise

If you fully obey the LORD your God and carefully follow all his commands I give you today, the LORD your God will set you high above all the nations on earth.

DEUTERONOMY 28:1 (NIV)

Blessings

Read Deuteronomy 28: 2-14 and answer the question that follows:

All these blessings will come upon you and accompany you if you obey the LORD your God:

You will be blessed in the city and blessed in the country.

The fruit of your womb will be blessed, and the crops of your land and the young of your livestock—the calves of your herds and the lambs of your flocks.

Your basket and your kneading trough will be blessed.

You will be blessed when you come in and blessed when you go out.

The LORD will grant that the enemies who rise up against you will be defeated before you. They will come at you from one direction but flee from you in seven.

The LORD will send a blessing on your barns and on everything you put your hand to.

The LORD your God will bless you in the land he is giving you.

The LORD will establish you as his holy people, as he promised you on oath, if you keep the commands of the LORD your God and walk in his ways. Then all the peoples on earth will see that you are called by the name of the LORD, and they will fear you.

The LORD will grant you abundant prosperity—in the fruit of your womb, the young of your livestock and the crops of your ground—in the land he swore to your forefathers to give you.

The LORD will open the heavens, the storehouse of his bounty, to send rain on your land in season and to bless all the work of your hands.

You will lend to many nations but will borrow from none.

The LORD will make you the head, not the tail. If you pay attention to the commands of the LORD your God that I give you this day and carefully follow them, you will always be at the top, never at the bottom.

Do not turn aside from any of the commands I give you today, to the right or to the left, following other gods and serving them.

Write, in your own words, the blessings God promises to those who obey His laws.

_____

_____

_____

_____

_____

_____

_____

_____

_____

_____

_____

_____

_____

_____

Curses

Now read Deuteronomy 28:15-68.

Sum up, in your own words, what curses will come upon those who do not follow God's commands.

_____

_____

_____

_____

_____

_____

_____

_____

Day 5

God originally established His covenant with Abraham in Genesis 12:1-3. It was fulfilled through Jesus Christ who established the new covenant by becoming a curse for us, which means that now anyone can enter into this same covenant by faith in Jesus Christ.

Reflect on Galatians 3:13-14 (NIV) and answer the questions.

Christ redeemed us from the curse of the law by becoming a curse for us, for it is written: "Cursed is everyone who is hung on a tree." He redeemed us in order that the blessing given to Abraham might come to the Gentiles through Christ Jesus, so that by faith we might receive the promise of the Spirit.

In your opinion, what does the "curse of the law" as described in Galatians 3:13 mean?

_____

_____

_____

_____

_____

What does it mean to you that Christ became the "curse for us"?

_____

_____

_____

_____

_____

_____

_____

We no longer have to suffer the curses under which the world's system operates. This same covenant and its blessings are available to you today. In Deuteronomy 30:11 God said, "Now what I am commanding you today is not too difficult for you or beyond your reach." It did turn out too hard for the Israelites to follow, which meant God had to establish this new covenant.

"The problem with the Old Covenant was not with God but rather with humanity," says Jim Cymbala in Fresh Power, "but rather with humanity, which was so ruined by sin that people were unable to keep God's holy commands no matter how hard they tried.... There was the need for a whole new arrangement on a totally different basis."

Reflect on the following Scriptures:

Deuteronomy 29:12-13 (NIV)

You are standing here in order to enter into a covenant with the LORD your God, a covenant the LORD is making with you this day and sealing with an oath, to confirm you this day as his people, that he may be your God as he promised you and as he swore to your fathers, Abraham, Isaac and Jacob.

Deuteronomy 30:19-20 (NIV)

This day I call heaven and earth as witnesses against you that I have set before you life and death, blessings and curses. Now choose life, so that you and your children may live and that you may love the LORD your God, listen to his voice, and hold fast to him. For the LORD is your life, and he will give you many years in the land he swore to give to your fathers, Abraham, Isaac and Jacob.

Ask God to show you what it will cost you if you choose life and live in His covenant, starting today.

_____

_____

_____

_____

_____

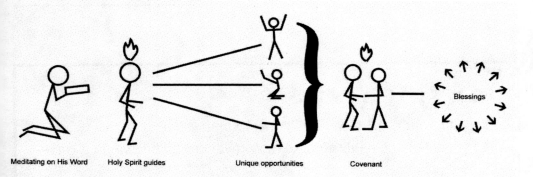

Meditating on His Word   Holy Spirit guides   Unique opportunities   Covenant   Blessings

System Guidance

Review today's lesson.

1. Prayerfully choose one statement or verse that was most meaningful to you today.

_____

_____

2. Write a prayer of response.

_____

_____

_____

_____

_____

_____

_____

_____

_____

_____

_____

_____

_____

_____

_____

3. What action do you need to take in response to today's lesson?

_____

_____

_____

_____

```
POWER POINTS
■ God's original covenant was with Abraham.
■ Jesus Christ established the new covenant by becoming a curse
  for us.
■ Anyone can enter into this new covenant by faith in Jesus Christ.
```

Journal

So shall My Word be that goes forth from My mouth. It shall not return to Me void, but it shall accomplish what I please. And it shall prosper in the thing for which I sent it.

Isaiah 55:11

OBSTACLES TO SUCCESSFUL FINANCIAL MANAGEMENT

It is unfortunate that our world does not view a person's strength based on spiritual vitality or moral character, but rather based on financial strength.

A few years ago I read an article in the *Ottawa Journal* about a couple who bought Kentucky Fried Chicken and went to a park to spend their lunch hour there. To their surprise, they found the money they had paid for the lunch in the bag. They went back immediately to return the money. The owner was overwhelmed by their honesty and wanted to make an example out of them. But when he asked them whether he could take their picture and have it published in the newspaper, they were horrified and begged the store owner not to do it, because they were both cheating on their spouses.

In sharp contrast to the get-rich-quick mentality that reigns in the world, God intends for us to work with integrity, keeping morality and truth in balance while pursuing true prosperity.

In your opinion, what is the world's view of finances?

_____

_____

How is this different from God's view?

_____

_____

Why do you think there is such a difference between the world's view and God's perspective on finances?

_____

_____

_____

_____

If your financial burden seems overwhelming, perhaps you are looking for a quick solution. Your needs may be very pressing. Still, it is imperative that we change our focus from self to God, our true Source of provision.

As Christians we are constantly challenged to live—and shine—in the midst of progressive darkness. We don't have the capacity to shine outside of God; we merely reflect His brilliance as we walk and commune with Him. Our walk cannot be impeded by broken principles like truth and integrity. There is no possibility for even the slightest compromise. We have to walk in God's truth and follow His laws in order to shine.

Have you broken any of God's principles or laws? Ask the Holy Spirit to reveal anything in your life that might not be in line with God's will and His Word.

_____

_____

_____

The world's plans don't require supernatural intervention and offer no real solution. On the other hand, God's plans are to prosper us, and not to harm us. His plans are to give us a hope and a future. But it does require that you choose to follow Him with your whole heart. God's design for your life requires His intervention in order to bring it to pass. Although He is concerned about your immediate needs, God knows that finding a permanent solution to your needs is a process. It is a journey.

We need to take steps to build our financial house on the solid Rock. Be sure to know that the storms will come, but if you are firmly established on the Rock, you will remain standing. Christ has overcome all these.

How committed are you to following God's instructions for your finances?

_____

_____

If you were to disagree with God's direction, what will you do?

_____

_____

_____

Are you prepared to adjust your life and have it line up with the Word of God? Write that into a statement.

_____

_____

_____

Some of the main factors that create lack and financial instability in our lives are the following:

- a compromised lifestyle
- deception
- comparing with others
- expecting quick results
- unrestrained desire
- spiritual laziness
- self-centered living

Is the Holy Spirit speaking to you about any of the above factors? What will you do about it?

_____

_____

_____

_____

_____

_____

_____

_____

_____

Reflect on Psalm 73:3

But as for me, my feet had almost slipped, I had nearly lost my foothold for I envied the arrogant when I saw the prosperity of the wicked.

Review today's lesson.

1. Prayerfully choose one statement or verse that was most meaningful to you today.

_____

_____

_____

2. Write a prayer of response.

_____

_____

_____

_____

_____

_____

_____

_____

_____

_____

3. What action do you need to take in response to today's lesson?

_____

_____

_____

POWER POINTS

- ■ Our faith walk cannot be impeded by broken principles like truth and integrity.
- ■ We have to walk in God's truth and follow His laws in order to shine for Him.
- ■ God's design for your life requires His intervention.
- ■ God is interested in finding a permanent solution to your needs.

SESSION 5
Day 6

ESSION VI

You

187

Not only so, but we also rejoice in our sufferings, because we know that suffering produces perseverance; perseverance, character; and character, hope; and hope does not disappoint us, because God has poured out his love into our hearts by the Holy Spirit, whom he has given us.

ROMANS 5:3-5 (NIV)

DEVELOPING CHARACTER FOR SUCCESS

It is sad that many Christians today thrive on God's love and grace without extending it to others. Paul wrote in 1 Corinthians 15:10, "But by the grace of God I am what I am, and His grace toward me was not in vain; but I labored more abundantly than they all, yet not I, but the grace of God which was with me."

The grace of God was priceless to early Christians and true seekers. But "grace" as a word has become cheap on the lips of many Christians. The root of the problem is our personal belief system—and not only in the mind, but in the heart also. Many have never taken time to interact with God, to really experience His love and grace, and then to pour it out.

We need to watch ourselves so that these kinds of false mind sets cannot come in to control our thoughts and make it impossible for faith to grow in our hearts.

There are four areas we have to watch:

1. Little vices or questionable lifestyles

Modern society continuously tries to desensitize us to so-called "little" sins. Having fun at any cost seems to be the ultimate gain. Material wealth is more important than moral character. A practicing Christian might become thoroughly convinced that in spite of little sins, like drinking, gambling, reckless driving, black and white lies, cheating in business, reading dirty literature, watching dirty TV materials, etc. that he is a good person at heart. In thinking this way, he completely fails to understand God's standard and view of sin. He does not realize that he has not entered into God's love and is in fact living under God's judgment.

J.I Packer writes: "Willingness to tolerate and indulge evil up to the limit is seen as a virtue, while living by fixed principles of right and wrong is censured by some as doubtfully moral. And unless one knows and feels the truth of this fact, that wrongdoers have no natural hope of anything from God but retributive judgment, one can never share the biblical faith in divine grace."

Where do you stand on the matter of little vices?

_____

_____

_____

_____

_____

_____

You are accountable to both yourself and to God. The results you see in your own life will be the guide to your progress. Your financial situation will change in proportion to your interaction with the Holy Spirit, your response to His promptings and your willingness to change.

2. Unforgiveness

Reflect on the following Scripture verses:

Mark 11:25-26
And whenever you stand praying, if you have anything against anyone, forgive him, that your Father in heaven may also forgive you your trespasses. But if you do not forgive, neither will your Father in heaven forgive your trespasses.

Matthew 18: 21-23
Then Peter came to Him and said, 'Lord, how often shall my brother sin against me, and I forgive him? Up to seven times?' Jesus said to him, 'I do not say to you, up to seven times, but up to seventy times seven. Therefore the kingdom of heaven is like a certain king who wanted to settle accounts with his servants.

Matthew 18:35
So My heavenly Father also will do to you if each of you, from his heart, does not forgive his brother his trespasses.

Forgiveness is a prerequisite for successful living. God gives us the ability to trust and have faith. When we do not forgive and live with unforgiveness

in our hearts, then faith will not be in us, because faith comes by continually hearing the Word of God.

Unforgiveness is a luxury of our flesh. Our spirit is crushed by providing this luxury to our flesh and maintaining it on an ongoing basis. However, when we start walking in the spirit, we will not fulfill the lust of the flesh. Unforgiveness breeds many other vices—including hardening the heart and bringing disaster in the financial realm. When we want to lead a successful life we cannot afford NOT to forgive, regardless of whose fault it is. Pride is the only thing that prevents people from forgiving others. God has established forgiveness as a law and nothing can change it.

Do you suffer the consequences of unforgiveness? If so, make a list of where you need to apply the healing balm of forgiveness.

_____

_____

_____

Ask God to give you the ability to deal with this area of your life.

_____

_____

_____

_____

_____

_____

3. Faith does not work outside of love.

Galatians 5:6

For in Christ Jesus neither circumcision nor uncircumcision avails anything, but faith working through love.

Let us guard ourselves of the mistaken idea that by believing God and developing faith in His Word, we can accomplish many things in our lives. God is all love and God is all faith. We need to receive the revelation that faith requires love to fulfill the promises of God; then we can have whatever we ask.

If we are going to examine ourselves on this line, we will be able to understand our unanswered prayer and struggles. The Bible says even demons believe and tremble before God, but they never receive anything from God because of the lack of love.

Meditate on the following verses of Scriptures and write down some key words to spark your memory:

Proverbs 10:12

_____

1 Peter 4:8

_____

Galatians 6:1

_____

1 Corinthians 13

_____

Philippians 2:3-4

_____

Romans 12:10

_____

4. Not Praying

We live in a real world with demons and evil spirits around us. Satan is their leader. He is the oldest copier that ever lived on this earth. He has studied each individual for the last 6,000 years. He knows all the tricks in this world—he invented most of them. He knows how we think, work and trust God. He accomplishes his task by deceiving us. We become pawns in his hand, and even work against ourselves. Our ignorance of satan and his workings keeps him safe and secure.

We may not like the idea of talking about evil, but it is a reality and we have to be aware of it. We cannot take part of God's Word and leave the other part. Our instructions are clear in the Bible about our dealing with satan and his demons.

Ephesians 6:10-17

Finally, my brethren, be strong in the Lord and in the power of His might.

Put on the whole armor of God, that you may be able to stand against the wiles of the devil. For we do not wrestle against flesh and blood, but against principalities, against powers, against the rulers of the darkness of this age, against spiritual hosts of wickedness in the heavenly places. Therefore take up the whole armor of God, that you may be able to withstand in the evil day, and having done all, to stand. Stand therefore, having girded your waist with truth, having put on the breastplate of righteousness, having shod your feet with the preparation of the gospel of peace; above all, taking the shield of faith with which you will be able to quench all the fiery darts of the wicked one. And take the helmet of salvation, and the sword of the Spirit, which is the word of God.

We are given very specific instructions regarding our action in response to the enemy: James 4:7 says, "Resist the devil, and he will flee from you."

When we receive God's revelation in these areas of our life, our progress will be swift. Our learning will not linger and if we have learned anything during the course of our lives that we will be able to apply, this understanding will come too. It is imperative that we press on and desire the presence of God in our lives more than anything else.

Review today's lesson.

1. Prayerfully choose one statement or verse that was most meaningful to you today.

_____

_____

_____

2. Write a prayer of response.

_____

_____

_____

_____

_____

_____

_____

_____

_____

3. What action do you need to take in response to today's lesson?

_____

_____

_____

_____

POWER POINTS

- Watch for little vices and ask God to keep you safe.
- Forgive and live in a continuous mode of forgiveness.
- Live in love and renew your mind daily.
- Watch, pray and put on the armour of God, so you won't be ignorant about the plans of the enemy.

Your Talents and Abilities

Your God-given abilities are tools to bring you prosperity. God is the Author and Creator of your talents. Every person has at least one talent. Most of us have a number of talents. It is our responsibility to discover them and use them to the glory of God. We are managers of these talents that were given to us by God.

When non-believers prosper, we may envy them, feel sorry for ourselves or blame God for not living up to His promises of providing our material needs. What often makes the difference between unbelievers who prosper, and believers who don't, is the way in which these individuals' talents are managed. The world seems to have a great awareness of talents and how to implement them for maximum benefit. Christians, on the other hand, tend to lean only on God's ability and love and often ignore their God-given abilities, thinking that to use them to make money, for example, might be a lower calling.

Instead of asking God to bless the things we want to do, we need to go to God, asking for a revelation of ourselves. When we understand how He has created us, we can understand the purpose He has for our lives. It happens far too often that we do things we were not supposed to do in the first place.

Read Exodus 35:30-35 and 36:1-7.

Why do you think God made man in His own image?

_____

_____

_____

God has made us His representatives on earth and ordained a destiny for each of us. He intends to work through human beings, assigning specific

> The man who had received the five talents brought the other five. "Master," he said, "you entrusted me with five talents. See I have gained five more."
>
> MATTHEW 25:20 (NIV)

195

responsibilities to specific individuals for His greater purpose. Our responsibility is to find out what that purpose is. When we do not consider the full calling of our lives we end up living at a much lower level than what God originally intended. God created this world for His pleasure and glory, but also for our enjoyment. God gives us our jobs and families, not only to glorify Him, but also that we may enjoy life.

Pray and ask the Holy Spirit to take you to the spiritual level where God wants you to be. Ask Him to explain to you today's Scriptures and how you can apply it to your own life.

Meditate on 3 John 2-4

Beloved, I pray that you may prosper in all things and be in health, just as your soul prospers. For I rejoiced greatly when brethren came and testified of the truth that is in you, just as you walk in the truth. I have no greater joy than to hear that my children walk in truth.

Why did God intend each of us to be prosperous in all things, and to be in good health, just as our souls prosper?

_____

_____

_____

_____

Recognizing your skills

Take a moment to reflect on Deuteronomy 8:18

And you shall remember the LORD your God, for it is He who gives you power to get wealth, that He may establish His covenant which He swore to your fathers, as it is this day.

In 1976, for the eleventh consecutive year, Joe Girard sold more automobiles and trucks on a one-to-one basis than in any other year. In 1973, Joe sold 1,425 cars and trucks, a world record which may never be broken. Joe is the only salesman listed in the business section of *The Guinness Book of World Records*. His commissions in 1975 totaled $191,000.00. He did not need any capital to make money. He made money out of his skill. He tapped into his God-given ability. You can do the same too but you have to find out what is your God-given ability.

What are your God-given abilities? List as many as you can think of.

_____

_____

_____

_____

_____

_____

What are you passionate about?

_____

_____

_____

What do you like to pursue in life?

_____

_____

_____

Review today's lesson.

1. Prayerfully choose one statement or verse that was most meaningful to you today.

_____

_____

_____

2. Write a prayer of response.

_____

_____

_____

_____

_____

_____

_____

_____

3. What action do you need to take in response to today's lesson?

_____

_____

_____

POWER POINTS

■ God works through people, assigning specific responsibilities to specific individuals for His greater purpose.

■ God intends for you to be prosperous in all things.

■ You can use your talents as tools for prosperity.

■ God is the Author and Creator of your talents.

■ You are a representative of God on earth, and You are responsible for sharing His plan with those who don't know Him yet.

Journal

BLESSED TO BE A BLESSING

Praise be to the God and Father of our Lord Jesus Christ, who has blessed us in the heavenly realms with every spiritual blessing in Christ.

EPHESIANS 1:3

I have tested and experienced the incredible truth of God's abundant blessir in my own life. In times of severe need and personal challenges, God m me and my needs both spiritually and materially. Once I learned to app God's principles in my life, they haven't failed, not even once.

But it wasn't always like that. Before I could experience God's miracle-workir power in my life, I had to learn and understand His principles. I was thrown in deep waters, but step by step the Holy Spirit led me through my circumstances a place where He could bless me. Under God's instruction, I began to swim. Gc also made it very clear that He blesses me so I can bless and teach others. Whe we learn God's ways, we need to apply them for the benefit of His Kingdom.

Once I learned and understood the principles of God's provision, my emotion and financial troubles did not disappear instantly, but I received wisdom to sta dealing with life and finances His way.

Your crop

Your workplace and your business is the grounds where you can produce crop Your crop may not literally be wheat or grain, but it is anything you are workin on. Thousands of possibilities of failure may surround that field. Similarl thousands of possibilities of gain and profit may surround it. Our fear is of th unknown future, of figurative roadblocks, of curves and turns.

When we develop a friendship with God and He becomes our Master, w develop confidence in His Word. He guides us, gives us instructions, and saves u from making wrong choices. He sharpens our listening faculties and we develo a listening skill in our spirit.

Day 3

Reflect on the following Scripture verse:

Malachi 3: 11 -12

And I will rebuke the devourer for your sakes, so that he will not destroy the fruit of your ground, nor shall the vine fail to bear fruit for you in the field," says the LORD of hosts. "And all nations will call you blessed, for you will be a delightful land," says the LORD of hosts.

_____

_____

_____

_____

Moving mountains

Reflect on Matthew 17:20.

So Jesus said to them, "Because of your unbelief; for assuredly, I say to you, if you have faith as a mustard seed, you will say to this mountain, 'Move from here to there,' and it will move; and nothing will be impossible for you."

The number one mountain in most people's lives, is dealing with finances. Most North Americans are buried under a mountain of debt and financial burdens. As children of God, we have an advantage over unbelievers in removing these mountains, because we can apply faith. But we also need to study the laws of God's abundant provision and operate within them, by faith.

What mountain in your life seems insurmountable at the moment?

_____

_____

_____

_____

What tool did Jesus tell His disciples to use for moving mountains? What does this mean to you?

_____

_____

_____

_____

Review today's lesson.

1. Prayerfully choose one statement or verse that was most meaningful to you today.

_____

_____

_____

2. Write a prayer of response.

_____

_____

_____

_____

_____

_____

_____

_____

_____

_____

_____

_____

3. What action do you need to take in response to today's lesson?

_____

_____

_____

POWER POINTS

- You can move financial mountains through faith.
- God's principles for success never fail.
- You are blessed so you may be a blessing to others.

 ournal

Dishonest money dwindles away, but he who gathers money little by little makes it grow.

PROVERBS 13:11

YOUR RELATIONSHIP WITH MONEY

Money needs a good manager. It really does not matter how much you have when you start your life with but rather what attitude you have towards money. By wisdom and following the right principles, many people have become successful with very little start-up money. Conversely a great number of people have lost their family heritage by mismanaging a large amount of money poorly.

Frustration, fear and failure may try to prevent you from living abundantly. To guard against distractions and falling into despair, set goals, know your worth as a creation of God, and strive for excellence in everything you do. Think positively, casting down any high thing that exalts itself above God's Word.

Reflect on Romans 15:17-18 (NLT):

So it is right for me to be enthusiastic about all Christ Jesus has done through me in my service to God. I dare not boast of anything else.

What do you think is the difference between confidence in self and confidence in God?

_____

_____

What does it mean to you to deny yourself?

_____

_____

While we are planning to live a long life we must die to self. Our financial success lies in managing ourselves and managing our money. People may have great ideas but a person who puts it into action reaps the benefits.

For a Christian, God is offering His help, His ideas, His blessings, His miracle-working power and His never-ending resources. We must ask

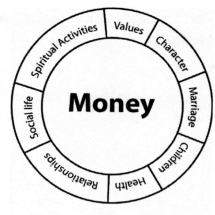

What is central in your life?

ourselves a question: Am I ready to accept His offer and His help in my financial matters or am I trying to prove that I can do it myself? In this way, I am not much more than one who denies God and sets out to do everything by herself. If you feel you want to do it on your own then perhaps it is time for self-examination. Why do you want to do it your own way?

Humility

Reflect on the following Scripture verses:

Proverbs 11:2 (NIV)
When pride comes, then comes disgrace, but with humility comes wisdom.

_____

_____

_____

Proverbs 15:33 (NIV)
The fear of the LORD teaches a man wisdom, and humility comes before honour.

_____

_____

_____

Wisdom starts with fear of the Lord and humility. Your financial desperate need will not open the door to God's supernatural intervention. But your humble cry for help will open His heart. Many fail to experience God's miracle-working power of God when they hang on to the facade of a rich lifestyle, while actually living in great need, both spiritually and financially. Don't let pride get in the way of experiencing all that God has for you.

Reflect on the following Scriptures and write them into your own statements:

Job. 35:12-13

There they cry out, but He does not answer, because of the pride of evil men. Surely God will not listen to empty talk, nor will the Almighty regard it.

_____

_____

_____

Proverbs 8:13

The fear of the LORD is to hate evil; pride and arrogance and the evil way and the perverse mouth I hate.

_____

_____

_____

Proverbs 11:2

When pride comes, then comes shame; but with the humble is wisdom.

_____

_____

_____

Proverbs 16:18

Pride goes before destruction, and a haughty spirit before a fall.

_____

_____

_____

Proverbs 29:23

A man's pride will bring him low, but the humble in spirit will retain honour.

_____

_____

_____

Obadiah 1:2-4

Behold, I will make you small among the nations; you shall be greatly despised. The pride of your heart has deceived you, you who dwell in the clefts of the rock, whose

habitation is high; you who say in your heart, 'Who will bring me down to the ground? Though you ascend as high as the eagle, and though you set your nest among the stars, from there I will bring you down,' says the LORD.

_____

_____

_____

1 John 2:16

For all that is in the world—the lust of the flesh, the lust of the eyes, and the pride of life is not of the Father but is of the world.

_____

_____

_____

Find a financial mentor

For your own long-term benefit, seek out the help and wisdom of experts. There are many Christian financial counselors who can help and guide you to put your financial affairs in the proper perspective. An outsider can usually give an unbiased opinion and help correct mistakes. In my own life when I tried to be all-knowing, I lost all the financial blessings God had given so freely.

Review today's lesson.

1. Prayerfully choose one statement or verse that was most meaningful to you today.

_____

_____

_____

2. Write a prayer of response.

_____

_____

_____

_____

_____

_____

3. What action do you need to take in response to today's lesson?

_____

_____

_____

POWER POINTS

■ Money requires a good manager.

■ God's Word offers balance.

■ It is best to have confidence in God's ability, not your own.

■ Seek out wise financial counsel.

 *J*ournal

WORRIES

Therefore I tell you, do not worry about your life, what your will eat; or about your body, what you will wear. Life is more than food, the body more than clothes ...Who of you by worrying can add a single hour to his life: Since you cannot do this very little thing, why do you worry about the rest ... your Father knows that you need them. But seek his kingdom, and these things will be given to you as well.

READ LUKE 12: 22 - 31

Worry is the opposite of trust. Worry has no faith and does not experience peace.

Hear the parable of two friends, John and Mark. When John came down with the flu, his friend Mark promised that he would come and take care of him as soon as he finished work. John knew Mark well, he trusted him and he slept in peace until Mark showed up at his door, just after 5pm.

Since John knew his friend, he did not worry. He did not have to have a back-up plan or call someone else. He did not worry about what he had to do in case Mark didn't show up.

This trust depended on how well the two friends knew each other. In the same way, our trust (or faith) in God grows as we come to know Him better and grow in our relationship with Him.

Worry breeds fear and destroys our faith in God. It brings sickness, division and even poverty.

How much do you worry?

_____

_____

_____

Do you remember a time when you were particularly anxious? When you worry, what kind of decisions do you make?

_____

_____

_____

_____

_____

_____

_____

_____

How do you deal with financial pressure?

_____

_____

_____

What did Jesus say about the pressures of daily life?

_____

_____

_____

What did Jesus say should we do in order to refrain from worrying? What does that mean to you?

_____

_____

_____

When you start cultivating knowledge about God and meditate on His Word day and night, you will make progress on the path of freedom from worries. Your financial situation might not change immediately, but as you give ownership of your life and your circumstances to God, He will lead you into your heritage as a child of the King.

Review today's lesson.

1. Prayerfully choose one statement or verse that was most meaningful to you today.

_____

_____

_____

2. Write a prayer of response.

_____

_____

_____

_____

_____

_____

3. What action do you need to take in response to today's lesson?

_____

_____

_____

_____

_____

_____

POWER POINTS

- ■ Worrying is the opposite of trusting.
- ■ Worry breeds fear.
- ■ Worries will destroy your faith in God.

Journal

TAKING ACTION

215

There is a time for everything, and a season for every activity under heaven.

ECCLESIASTES 3:1 (NIV)

TIME MANAGEMENT

Time is a gift from God. How you use it is your choice. You can plant time as seeds and receive a great harvest. Time is limited. You cannot buy it and you cannot increase it. It is allotted to us by God, but we ourselves have to manage it. You can invest time, you can use it or you can waste it.

In reality time is money. The more time you put in work, the more money you make. The more time you put in anything will result in a commensurate and proportionate return.

The world offers many time-management programs. Big corporations spend thousands of dollars to teach employees effective time management skills. Why? Because productivity is the name of the game. And if employees are managing their time well, the corporation's profit margins soar.

In a Christian's life, eternity is supposed to be the highest priority. We can shape our eternal future by means of our time and money. God has made us stewards of our time. For purposeful, specific use of time, consider these three simple steps:

1. Decide on a specific time to pray.
2. Make your prayers specific.
3. Find a quiet place to spend your prayer time.

There are 96 fifteen-minute periods every day. Can you allot one or two of these time periods to God? It is your responsibility to plan and cultivate a prayer life. If you are just starting your prayer life then it will be hard to pray even for five minutes. If you find it hard to stay focused, try and pray the following Scriptures: Psalms 91, 23, and 103.

What are the obstacles to starting a disciplined prayer life?

_____

_____

Make a practical list and timetable to help you establish your own prayer discipline.

_____

_____

_____

_____

_____

_____

_____

_____

_____

_____

Why we should pray consistently

When we pray we are not trying to influence God to answer our prayers or feel sorry for our financial situations. We pray because we believe God and we stand against satan's plans to destroy us. Satan does not want us to fulfill our God-given destinies. God has given us everything that can bless us and make us a blessing to others. Satan is against our prosperity, our children, our marriage, our health and our lifestyles which means that we have to put on the armour of God daily. Don't leave home without it!

Douglas Steere, a great man of God says, "It is in prayer that you can face temptation and recognize your peculiar weakness at the moment it threatens to overwhelm you. If we stay in prayer we are given the strength needed to refuse the temptation so that we are no longer helplessly vulnerable to it."

Here are some wonderful promises from God to help kickstart your prayer life:

Promises for your unsaved loved ones

Acts 16:31, Acts 11:14, 1 Peter 3:1-2, 1 Corinthians 7:13-16, Romans 5:8, 2 Peter 3:9, John 3:17, Luke 5:32

Promises for your children

Isaiah 54:13, Psalm 127:3-5, Psalm 8:2, Colossians 3:20, Proverbs 22:6, Isaiah 44:3, Psalm 91:11-12, 2 Timothy 3:15, Isaiah 49:25, Proverbs 3:4

Promises for prosperity

Philippians 4:19, Psalm 34:10, Psalm 37:25, Psalm 23:1-3 John 2, Matthew 6:31-33, Luke 6:38, 2 Corinthians 9:6-8

Promises for healing

James 5:14-16, Hebrews 13:8, Malachi 4:2, Mark 16:15-18, Psalm 103:3, 3 John 2, Isaiah 53:5, Matthew 9:35, Jeremiah 17:14, Luke 6:19, Jeremiah 30:17, Exodus 15:26, Proverbs 4:20-22, Psalm 107:20, Matthew 8:8

Review today's lesson.

1. Prayerfully choose one statement or verse that was most meaningful to you today.

_____

_____

_____

2. Write a prayer of response.

_____

_____

_____

_____

_____

_____

_____

_____

3. What action do you need to take in response to today's lesson?

_____

_____

_____

POWER POINTS

- Time is a gift from God.
- Time is limited.
- Consistently set aside time every day to talk to God.
- Put on the armour of God daily.
- Pray in faith, standing with God against satan's evil plans to destroy you.

The effective, fervent prayer of a righteous man avails much.

JAMES 5:16

LIVING A BALANCED LIFE

When you make the decision to lead an obedient life you will face a crisis of faith. During this time Satan will try to destroy your newfound faith by creating imbalance in your prayer and giving.

Between prayer and giving in the Christian world, prayer has received the hardest blows. A writer reflects, "As poor as our giving is, our contributions of money exceed our offerings of prayer. Perhaps in the average congregation fifty aid in paying, where one saintly ardent soul shuts himself up with God and wrestles for deliverance of the heathen world."

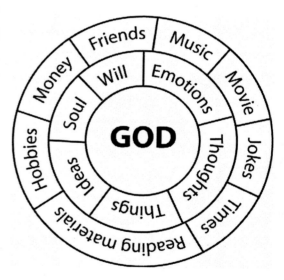

How often people have said, "Prayer may be fine, but I will work instead. Somebody has to get the job done."

However without constant prayer and active faith in the Word of God we cannot receive the fullness of either the soul harvest or the financial harvest. It is easy to sow our money and then sit back and wait for the harvest to come in. It won't happen. It does not happen in the natural crop nor will it happen in the spiritual crop.

God's Word warns us about this in Mark 4:3-8.

Listen! Behold, a sower went out to sow. And it happened, as he sowed, that some seed fell by the wayside; and the birds of the air came and devoured it. Some fell on stony ground, where it did not have much earth; and immediately it sprang up because it had no depth of earth. But when the sun was up it was scorched, and because it had no root it withered away. And some seed fell among thorns; and the thorns grew up

and choked it, and it yielded no crop. But other seed fell on good ground and yielded a crop that sprang up, increased and produced: some thirty fold, some sixty, and some a hundred.

As soon as the sower went out to sow the seeds he faced problems. Jesus said the problems will come. Even Christians who sincerely seek to find the will of God fail to see the need for a proper balance between prayer and work. It is a proven fact that in Christian history those who were most successful, prayed most. Those who pray most work the best.

Martin Luther, when asked about his plans for tomorrow answered: "Work, work, and more work from early until late. In fact, I have so much to do that I shall spend the first three hours in prayer."

How much time do you spend daily before you prepare to face your day?

_____

_____

_____

Is it possible that God might be talking to you about your prayer life? What do you think is He saying?

_____

_____

_____

According to Mark 4: 3-8, when is trouble time?

_____

_____

_____

What kind of practical changes are you prepared to make in your prayer life?

_____

_____

_____

God told the Jews that their new land, flowing with milk and honey, could not be occupied without a fight. Egypt was not the same as the land He had promised them. Egypt represents our lives lived under the bondage of sin. Through faith in Christ we came out of Egypt and are on our way to the Promised Land.

Read Deuteronomy 11:8-12

When there were hard times in the wilderness, the Jews complained and wanted to go back to Egypt. It cost them their lives and only the next generation was allowed to enter the Promised Land. They failed to enjoy the pleasure of the land and never experienced the success God had in store for them. Similarly, when we run into hardship in our Christian walk, we must not complain, otherwise we might have to stay in the wilderness for a long time. But if we walk with God, we can experience the abundant life Christ promised right now. Although the Promised Land is full of hills and valleys, it is governed by the promises of God.

Read the following Scriptures and respond to the questions:

Ephesians 6:10-11

Finally, my brethren, be strong in the Lord and in the power of His might. Put on the whole armor of God, that you may be able to stand against the wiles of the devil.

Who needs to be strong and prepare to face the enemy?

_____

_____

_____

Ephesians 6:12

For we do not wrestle against flesh and blood, but against principalities, against powers, against the rulers of the darkness of this age, against spiritual hosts of wickedness in the heavenly places.

Who is our enemy? What kind of enemy is he?

_____

_____

_____

_____

Ephesians 6:13-14

Therefore take up the whole armor of God, that you may be able to withstand in the evil day, and having done all, to stand. Stand therefore, having girded your waist with truth, having put on the breastplate of righteousness.

Who is going to stand in the evil days? How long will it last?

_____

_____

_____

Why is it important to stand?

_____

_____

_____

_____

Ephesians 6:15-16

... and having shod your feet with the preparation of the gospel of peace; above all, taking the shield of faith with which you will be able to quench all the fiery darts of the wicked one.

What are the enemy's arrows aiming for?

_____

What is the shield of faith?

_____

_____

Where and how do you get it?

_____

_____

Ephesians 6:17-18

And take the helmet of salvation, and the sword of the Spirit, which is the word of God; praying always with all prayer and supplication in the Spirit, being watchful to this end with all perseverance and supplication for all the saints.

Why do you think it is hard for a Christian to obtain financial success?

_____

_____

_____

_____

_____

_____

Why it is important to pray?

_____

_____

_____

_____

How much should you pray?

_____

_____

1 Corinthians 2: 4-5

And my speech and my preaching were not with persuasive words of human wisdom, but in demonstration of the Spirit and of power, that your faith should not be in the wisdom of men but in the power of God.

On what should we base our faith? And what not?

_____

_____

_____

Isaiah 7: 9b

If you will not believe, surely you shall not be established...

What is the danger of not believing?

_____

_____

_____

Hebrews 11:6

But without faith it is impossible to please Him, for he who comes to God must believe that He is, and that He is a rewarder of those who diligently seek Him.

What is God's purpose in commanding us to believe in Him and have faith?

_____

_____

_____

_____

Spend the Time

A crucial lesson we must learn in prayer is the proper use of time. We live in a busy era where a strange paradox occurs: we work hard, yet accomplish little.

One writer has said, "In this restless and busy age most of us live too much in public. We spend our spiritual strength and forget to renew it. We multiply engagement and curtail our prayers. By an error of judgment, or perhaps by subtle force of inclination, which we mistake for necessity, we work when we ought to pray, because to an active mind work is far easier than prayer."

Luther knew that prayer paves the highway to accomplishment. To this end he prayed often and hard. Through prayer and Bible study Luther learned about satan's goal in fighting warriors of prayer. Satan tries to make us think we pray too much and work too little.

Christians will progress towards healthy financial lives only when we learn the need for work combined with prayer. This is a crisis of belief we must overcome in order to be productive in our homes and in God's Kingdom.

Ecclesiastes 3:1-4

To everything there is a season, a time for every purpose under heaven: a time to be born, and a time to die; a time to plant, and a time to pluck what is planted; a time to kill, and a time to heal; a time to break down, and a time to build up; a time to weep, and a time to laugh; a time to mourn, and a time to dance...

Have you experienced a season of prayer in your life? If yes, write down the outcome of that prayer season.

_____

_____

_____

_____

SESSION 7

Day 2

If you have not experienced a prayer season in your life, do you think God is calling you to invest time in it?

_____

_____

When and how can you start?

_____

_____

Review today's lesson.

1. Prayerfully choose one statement or verse that was most meaningful to you today.

_____

_____

2. Write a prayer of response.

_____

_____

3. What action do you need to take in response to today's lesson?

_____

_____

POWER POINTS
- ■ Prayer is your first seed towards financial breakthrough.
- ■ Pray with purpose.
- ■ When God works with me He requires faith.
- ■ Satan will come immediately to try and kill your faith.
- ■ God is a rewarder of those who diligently seek Him.
- ■ God will do His part, when you do yours.

*J*ournal

THE TURNING POINT

nvite God to join in your financial planning, decision-making and spendir How can we do that in a practical way? The first seed you plant is that prayer. Cultivate an effective prayer life. It has nothing to do with how de you are in debt or how little you have. Change our financial situations in t spiritual realm first and then it will manifest itself in the physical realm.

1 John 5:14-15

Now this is the confidence that we have in Him, that if we ask anything according to F will, He hears us. And if we know that He hears us, whatever we ask, we know that ; have the petitions that we have asked of Him.

Once you have decided to make prayer a part of your life, proceed to form habit of prayer. An author once commented, "A habit has been defined as an a repeated so often that it becomes involuntary. There is no new decision of mir each time the act is performed. Jesus prayed. He loved to pray. Often praying w; His way of resting. He prayed so often it became part of His life."

The early church nurtured the habit of prayer because they found no oth way to win the holy war. They considered prayer as serious business in followir Christ.

It does not matter how long you have been a Christian, if you have not plante your prayer as seeds, please take up this challenge and start today.

How often do you pray? Be honest.

_____

_____

_____

_____

Therefore I say to you, whatever things you ask when you pray, believe that you receive them, and you will have them.

MARK 11:24

Describe in your own words the importance of prayer as seed.

_____

_____

_____

_____

_____

_____

_____

Real Stories

Bishop Ashbury, a famous saint of God, related, "I propose to rise at four o'clock as often as I can and spend two hours in prayer and meditation."

It is said about Joseph Alleine, another giant of God's Word, that when four o'clock arrived, he began to pray and continued until eight o'clock.

Dr. Adoniram Judson, a giant for God, spoke clearly on the values of creating prayer habits: "Arrange thy affairs, if possible, so that thou canst leisurely devote two or three hours every day not merely to devotional exercises but to the very act of secret prayer and communion with God."

Sir Henry Havelock had a habit of welcoming each day with two hours of prayerful solitude. When he had to leave home at six o'clock he would rise from sleep two hours earlier for his prayer time.

Stonewall Jackson fastened firmly in his mind the habit of prayer. He said, "I have fixed the habit in my mind that I never raise a glass of water to my lips without asking God's blessing, never seal a letter without putting a word of prayer under the seal, never take a letter from the post without a brief sending of my thoughts heavenward, never change my classes in the lecture room without a minute's petition for the cadets who go out and for those who come in."

S.D. Gordon adds this insight: "The first thing in prayer is to find God's purpose, the trend, the swing of it; the second thing to make that purpose our prayer." Gordon continues, "Now prayer is this: finding God's purpose for our lives, and for the earth, and insisting that it shall be done here. The great thing then is to find out and insist upon God's will. And the how of method in prayer is concerned with that."

These are only a few examples of modern men to encourage you. It is possible to develop an effective prayer life. We can do it only when we realize the importance of it and its impact on our lives. In the above Scripture verse John is talking about the confidence we have in God that whatever we ask according to His will, He will give it to us. This should be our foundation.

After reading the above commitment to prayer from ordinary people who did extraordinary things for God, what changes should you make in your prayer life?

_____

_____

_____

_____

_____

_____

What discourages you to pray?

_____

_____

_____

An Action Plan

George Muller, a giant of faith and prayer, started his day by first talking to God. God found a man who listened to Him and then did His will. God found a steward who left a mark in the world. He was an ordinary man. He was not wealthy nor did he have any organization behind him to support him and yet he provided for more than 2,000 orphans in England.

We can learn from Muller's six-point plan to knowing and understanding God's will. We can apply his principles to building our financial freedom and being the steward God requires each of us to be.

1. I seek at the beginning to get my heart into such a state that it has no will of its own in regard to a given matter.

2. Having done this, I do not leave the result to feelings or simple impressions. If I do so, I make myself liable to great delusions.

3. I seek the will of the Spirit through, or in connection with, the Word of God.

4. Next I take into account providential circumstances. These often plainly indicate God's will in connection with His Word and Spirit.

5. I ask God in prayer to reveal His will to me aright.

6. Thus, through prayer to God, the study of the Word, and reflection, I come to a deliberate judgment according to the best of my ability and knowledge.

By following these simple but profound truths, he achieved the highest heights in Christian service and left a model for us to learn from. Reflect the six-point plan and you can implement it in your own life. Muller did everything with purpose. He had a goal. He did not passively wait on God for indefinite periods of time.

Personalize Muller's six steps and write them in your own words.

_____

_____

_____

_____

What part of Muller's six steps is most needed in your life right now?

_____

_____

_____

Are you fearful of taking action after prayer?

_____

_____

Consider point six and write your own action statement.

_____

_____

POWER POINTS
- Every faith giant in history has also been a prayer giant.
- Prayer is finding God's purpose for your life, and for the earth, and insisting that it shall be done here.
- When you come before God in prayer, bring your heart into such a state that it has no will of its own in regards to your request.

Journal

TAKING ACTION

Our financial prosperity is not a destination, but a journey. Learning God's principles and applying those principles in our life requires prayer, faith and patience. Once we understand this truth we won't get tired of doing the same thing every day. We will be diligent in prayer. We will work and strive for excellence, continuously seeking to improve ourselves. The battle for financial success will never be over unless and until we realize that we may have success because of Jesus.

James 1:5-9

If any of you lacks wisdom, let him ask of God, who gives to all liberally and without reproach, and it will be given to him. But let him ask in faith, with no doubting, for he who doubts is like a wave of the sea driven and tossed by the wind. For let not that man suppose that he will receive anything from the Lord; he is a double-minded man, unstable in all his ways.

Ask God right now to give you an extra portion of wisdom.

_____
_____
_____
_____
_____
_____

What do you want out of life?

_____
_____
_____
_____
_____
_____

Blessed is the man who walks not in the counsel of the ungodly, nor stands in the path of sinners, nor sits in the seat of the scornful; But his delight is in the law of the LORD, and in His law he meditates day and night. He shall be like a tree planted by the rivers of water, that brings forth its fruit in its season, whose leaf also shall not wither; and whatever he does shall prosper.

PSALM 1:1-3

233

The Action Plan

Reflect on the following Scripture verse:

James 1:22-25

But be doers of the word, and not hearers only, deceiving yourselves. For if anyone is a hearer of the word and not a doer, he is like a man observing his natural face in a mirror; for he observes himself, goes away, and immediately forgets what kind of man he was. But he who looks into the perfect law of liberty and continues in it, and is not a forgetful hearer but a doer of the work, this one will be blessed in what he does.

_____

_____

_____

_____

_____

_____

_____

_____

The redeemed financial life is intimately connected with the spiritual life. First, you need to determine all that God wants to do through you. Second, you need to count what it will cost you. Then you need to divide your life into three parts:

1. What would you like to accomplish in your lifetime?

_____

_____

_____

2. What kind of steward would you like to be?

_____

_____

_____

3. What kind of legacy do you want to leave for your children and grandchildren?

_____

_____

Decision

Each individual has to deal with the decision-making process. Your decisions will either take you to high places, or bring you into the valley of despair and defeat.

James 3:13-17

Who is wise and understanding among you? Let him show by good conduct that his works are done in the meekness of wisdom. But if you have bitter envy and self-seeking in your hearts, do not boast and lie against the truth. This wisdom does not descend from above, but is earthly, sensual, demonic. For where envy and self-seeking exist, confusion and every evil thing are there. But the wisdom that is from above is first pure, then peaceable, gentle, willing to yield, full of mercy and good fruits, without partiality and without hypocrisy.

_____

_____

_____

Planned stewardship

Establish a financial relationship with God. This is your platform from which to build your dreams, aspirations and success. God has already made the covenant with you to bless you and prosper you. He even promises to give you wisdom if you ask Him. James 1:5 says, "If any of you lacks wisdom, let him ask of God, who gives to all liberally and without reproach, and it will be given to him. But let him ask in faith."

God is more interested in your success than you are, because you are His representative on this earth. You carry His image and you are His child. Have confidence in His personality. Be practical, but have a spiritual attitude.

Write down your present income and how much it will cost you to bring tithes and offerings to God.

_____

_____

What will the effects be on your present lifestyle and future plans?

_____

_____

What do you want to do with your offerings?

_____

_____

_____

How can you start depending on the Lord?

_____

_____

_____

Stewards do not dream up their own dreams but they implement the dreams of their master. It is important to renew your mind with the Word of God and keep a vigil to change continuously. In your journal make a page entitled "before" and another page for "after." On the "before" page, write: "I used to make my own plans and my own financial choices, then went to ask God to bless me." On the "after" page write: "I now set out to understand God's Word. I pray and ask God for His wisdom to lead me to the plan which He has ordained for me." Now watch and pray, asking God to reveal to you His plan. Write down anything He says.

Review today's lesson.

1. Prayerfully choose one statement or verse that was most meaningful to you today.

_____

_____

_____

2. Write a prayer of response.

_____

_____

_____

_____

_____

_____

_____

_____

3. What action do you need to take in response to today's lesson?

_____

_____

_____

POWER POINTS

- ■ Commit to following God's financial plan for your life.
- ■ Start keeping account of your giving.
- ■ Give in faith and with purpose.
- ■ How you live reveals how much you trust the Lord.

COUNT YOUR MONEY

Action Plan

Reflect on the following Scriptures:

James 2:14-17

What does it profit, my brethren, if someone says he has faith but does not have works? Can faith save him? If a brother or sister is naked and destitute of daily food, and one of you says to them, "Depart in peace, be warmed and filled," but you do not give them the things which are needed for the body, what does it profit? Thus also faith by itself, if it does not have works, is dead.

_____

_____

_____

_____

James 2:20-26

But do you want to know, O foolish man, that faith without works is dead? Was not Abraham our father justified by works when he offered Isaac his son on the altar? Do you see that faith was working together with his works, and by works faith was made perfect? And the Scripture was fulfilled which says, "Abraham believed God, and it was accounted to him for righteousness." And he was called the friend of God. You see then that a man is justified by works, and not by faith only. Likewise, was not Rahab the harlot also justified by works when she received the messengers and sent them out another way? For as the body without the spirit is dead, so faith without works is dead also.

_____

_____

_____

I have told you these things, so that in me you may have peace. In this world you will have trouble. But take heart! I have overcome the world.

JOHN 16:33 (NIV)

Start right where you are with your finances. It is foolish to wait for a while until you may have a little more and then start. Faith is now; it is in the present tense. Trust God now. He requires order in every area of our lives. The whole universe declares His orderly way of doing things. He has equipped us with sound minds and knowledge of His Word to start living life intelligently and He has given His Word to protect and lead us.

Start counting your money

Start with an operating budget. Make lists of the following:

1. Your monthly expenses
2. Urgent needs.
3. Education expenses
4. Vacation expenses
5. Transportation expenses
6. Future desires expenses

Prepare your budget according to your family's requirements. Try and include any future dreams you might have.

_____
_____
_____
_____
_____
_____
_____
_____
_____
_____
_____
_____

Crisis of belief

As soon as you write a budget or start planning for your future financial security, you will run into a crisis of belief. Your present needs may even overtake your present earnings. The figures might look overwhelming. Your mind may suggest to find another job, while the word "impossible" might flash through your head. To tip the scale in your favour, you need faith and God's guidance. What you will do next will reflect your trust in God and His Word.

To proceed along this journey I suggest drafting a budget, taking account of your most important items of life first, and urgent needs next. This has to be done in prayer, to receive God's guidance and His revelation of what is important and what really is urgent in your life at this time. Judge your priorities from God's point of view. You have to be sure that God is leading you. Each one of us will listen differently to God. Our outcome will be different. There is absolutely no set formula in the Kingdom of God. No two persons are alike; even our fingerprints are all different. In the same way, there is no one-size-fits-all financial package that will suit everyone's needs. The only thing that is the same, is our foundation on the Word of God and His principles of financial planning. Our God-given uniqueness will bring different results.

Reflect on the following Scriptures and write them into your own statements.

Proverbs 3:6
In all your ways acknowledge Him, and He shall direct your paths.

_____

_____

_____

Proverbs 16: 7
When a man's ways please the LORD, he makes even his enemies to be at peace with him.

_____

_____

_____

Proverbs 16:2
All the ways of a man are pure in his own eyes, but the LORD weighs the spirits.

_____

_____

_____

Isaiah 55:8

For My thoughts are not your thoughts, nor are your ways My ways,' says the LORD.

_____

_____

_____

What is your greatest fear at this point?

_____

_____

_____

What do you think is achievable and what not?

_____

_____

_____

Make a list what you cannot do and then what you can do, with God's guidance and help.

_____

_____

_____

Whenever you face a financial crisis, if you allow yourself to think clearly, it is seldom about money; instead it usually points to your faith. What you believe about God will determine your point of action.

Today, why not invite God to partner with you in your financial affairs? He will challenge you to God-sized tasks that you won't be able to accomplish in your own wisdom and intelligence. You will need His complete input and help. Partnering with God will demand a lifelong commitment. But the dividends are heavenly.

Review today's lesson.

1. Prayerfully choose one statement or verse that was most meaningful to you today.

_____

_____

2. Write a prayer of response.

_____

_____

_____

_____

_____

_____

_____

_____

_____

3. What action do you need to take in response to today's lesson?

_____

_____

_____

_____

POWER POINTS

- Invite God to be your partner.
- Involve Him in all financial decisions.
- Arrange your priorities according to His instructions.
- When you choose to follow God, you will face God-sized challenges.
- Once you make a decision, you will face a crisis of faith.
- Your life speaks for your decisions.

*J*ournal

DEALING WITH OPPOSITION

There is a conflict between soul (your mind, will and emotions) and spirit. The only way to deal with this conflict is by the Word of God. These conflicts are harsh and ruthless, and very destructive to the spiritual man. The reason these conflicts occur, is because the spirit wants to listen to God while the soul wants to operate according to the instructions it receives from the world.

Satan knows that man is weak and vulnerable in the area of trusting God, since we do not see God or talk to Him directly. But because our God is Spirit, we need to deal with Him in the spirit also.

The Bible says that "without faith it is impossible to please God." God has given us His Word which represents His self-existent quality and He expects His creation to trust Him and obey His instruction. It is not because He wants to demand our respect; it is for our protection against the evil one who rules this world and holds the power to destroy us.

It is important to understand that we share the planet with the enemy of our souls—Satan. He is also a spirit and has many demons that continuously challenge us and try to control us through deception and manipulation. Although he's constantly walking around, looking for ways to destroy us, God instructed us in detail how to deal with this part of our dilemma. Ephesians 6:11-12 says, "Put on the whole armor of God, that you may be able to stand against the wiles of the devil. For we do not wrestle against flesh and blood, but against principalities, against powers, against the rulers of the darkness of this age, against spiritual hosts of wickedness in the heavenly places."

By knowing the Word of God we can resist the devil and deal with the affairs of life wisely. In order to accomplish our task on earth successfully, and

> We know that the law is spiritual; but I am unspiritual, sold as a slave to sin. I do not understand what I do. For what I want to do I do not do, but what I hate I do.
>
> ROMANS 7:14 (NIV)

see results, we must renew our minds daily with the Word of God.

Read Psalm 91:1-6

He who dwells in the secret place of the Most High shall abide under the shadow of the Almighty. I will say of the Lord, "He is my refuge and my fortress; my God, in Him I will trust." Surely He shall deliver you from the snare of the fowler and from the perilous pestilence. He shall cover you with His feathers, and under His wings you shall take refuge; his truth shall be your shield and buckler. You shall not be afraid of the terror by night, nor of the arrow that flies by day, nor of the pestilence that walks in darkness, nor of the destruction that lays waste at noonday.

When God is your refuge and your fortress, and when you trust in Him, your soul will communicate with your spirit. And your spirit will effectively receive instruction from the Holy Spirit and you will be able to handle your worldly affairs with wisdom in order to achieve your God-given potential. Success will be inevitable.

Reflect on Philippians 4:6-8

Be anxious for nothing, but in everything by prayer and supplication, with thanksgiving, let your requests be made known to God; and the peace of God, which surpasses all understanding, will guard your hearts and minds through Christ Jesus. Finally, brethren, whatever things are true, whatever things are noble, whatever things are just, whatever things are pure, whatever things are lovely, whatever things are of good report, if there is any virtue and if there is anything praiseworthy—meditate on these things.

Instructions from Philippians 4:6-8:

- Be anxious for nothing.
- Pray for everything and make your requests known to God.
- God's peace will guard your mind from anxious thought
- Meditate on things that are true, noble, just, pure, lovely, of good report, virtuous and praiseworthy.
- Guard your mind—it is the battlefield of victory or defeat.

Taking note of your surroundings

We live in a hostile world, surrounded by fear, restlessness and hopelessness. The stories of Abraham and Lot have a lot to teach us about how society influences our lives and our families.

Read Genesis 18 and 19.

How was Lot affected by his surroundings?

_____

_____

_____

What was the difference between Abraham and Lot's choices?

_____

_____

_____

While Satan uses deception, the Holy Spirit convicts us of the Father's will and purposes—plans that are much higher than our own. Satan's plans for us are to destroy us, but with the help of the Holy Spirit, we can live above the corrupted world system.

Read the following Scripture and write down the steps you can take to enter into a God-controlled life.

2 Corinthians 10:5
Casting down arguments and every high thing that exalts itself against the knowledge of God, bringing every thought into captivity to the obedience of Christ.

1. _____

_____

2. _____

_____

3. _____

_____

Review today's lesson.

1. Prayerfully choose one statement or verse that was most meaningful to you today.

_____

_____

_____

_____

2. Write a prayer of response.

_____
_____
_____
_____
_____
_____
_____
_____
_____
_____
_____

3. What action do you need to take in response to today's lesson?

_____
_____
_____
_____

POWER POINTS

- There is conflict between soul and spirit.
- The only way to deal with conflict between spirit and soul is by the Word of God.
- In order to successfully accomplish your task on earth renew your mind daily with the Word of God.
- Satan uses deception.
- The Holy Spirit will convict you of God's will and purpose.

Journal

Conclusion

We have but scratched the surface of financial planning and yet we have seen how absolutely essential it is for us as Christians to be good stewards of God's resources and thereby share in the reward the Lord has for us, on earth as well as in heaven.

As children, did we not want to please our parents and bask in their favour when we did well? Did we not want to make them proud of us, and show them how capable we were and that we could be trusted? It is no different today when we look at our relationship with God. As Christians we want to carry out our stewardship responsibilities so that when our time comes, our Father might say "Well done good and faithful servant! You have been faithful with a few things; I will put you in charge of many things. Come and share in your master's happiness."

For a committed Christian it is very important to be judged favourably when meeting our Lord. To do so is evidence that we have lived the spiritual life, and shared in its bountiful fruits.

The most important thing to do is start on a plan. Speak to God, find out what you're supposed to do. Set your goals accordingly. Trust that if you make the first step and are committed to staying the course, God will work with you and do His part. Do not strive for perfection. Any plan is better than no plan. With time you will become better at not only planning, but also executing your plan. All God wants is a commitment and a willing heart. We are called to live the Christian life—to live our faith and turn that faith into action.

No matter how difficult your financial problems, or how hopeless the future might look to you at this time, it is a lot brighter than you can imagine. All it takes is faith and a willingness to act. You already know that to continue doing the same old thing will produce the same results. A fresh start with a positive frame of mind, and deciding on a strategy will give God the opportunity to work miracles in your life.

Remember the story of the mustard seed? From small beginnings great things can evolve.

With much love in Christ,

Indira

SOME BASICS ABOUT FINANCIAL PLANNING AND INVESTING

by George A Pedersson
Business Economist and Capital Market Strategist

In this section we will deal with a few basic aspects of financial planning and investing from a biblical perspective. Financial planning can be a complex and intimidating exercise. Because most people believe this to be the case, they are intimidated and don't attempt a financial plan for themselves or their household. People are intimidated.

There is also a perception that to have a financial plan is to lose control of your life and decisions, being forced to adjust your future to a pre-conceived plan. This, we rationalize, takes the fun and excitement out of living. Nothing could be further from the truth.

Let us try and put financial planning in perspective, and look at some of its most basic elements, so as to see the benefits and freedom it gives.

What is Financial Planning?

Ron Blue, a well-known U.S. Christian financial planner and philanthropist has two easy-to-understand definitions of financial planning.

The more general description is:

Financial planning is the pre-determined use of financial resources in order to accomplish certain goals and objectives.

This definition assumes the person or household has some specific goals or objectives to be achieved over some time horizon. Some examples of goals or objectives may be:

1. To accumulate a downpayment for a home.

2. To pay off a mortgage as fast as possible.

3. To save for a new car.

4. To put aside enough money for a child's education.

5. To pay off all non-mortgage debt in a certain number of years.

6. To save for a memorable family vacation every five years.

7. To be debt free.

8. To save enough money for retirement so that a specific standard of living can be enjoyed.

9. To build wealth so that it can be used for the Great Commission.

The list of goals and objectives are endless. They will be unique to the specific desires and needs of each individual and household. To the extent we have goals or objectives, and truly desire to achieve them, it follows that the way in which we manage finances can either work to accomplish them, or on the contrary, to sabotage them.

If we truly wish to accomplish a set of goals, then it makes sense to look ahead and identify the types of activities, which use financial resources, that are consistent with achieving the goals, and which ones are inconsistent. This brings us to Ron Blue's other definition:

Financial planning is allocating limited financial resources among various unlimited alternatives.

There are only five basic uses of money:

1. Give it away

2. Pay down debt

3. Pay taxes

4. Support a lifestyle

5. Savings/investment

Importantly all of these uses of money are mutually exclusive. Within each use there are many alternatives. Therefore, to the extent we use financial resources in any of these five ways, they either support or subvert the goals or objectives we have.

Is financial planning and money relevant for a Christian? Are we not to rely on the Lord to provide for us as stated in Luke 12:22-31.

Money, and how it is used is important for Christians. Money is a subject cited in more scriptures than any other subject. That has to tell us something, but what?

Ron Blue has distilled four basic biblical principles of money management, or financial planning in a broader sense. These are essential for a Christian to understand and apply so that he or she can lead a fulfilling life, free from the anxiety that seems to pre-occupy so many of us. The key parable in the Bible is the parable of the talents in Matthew.

1. God Owns It All

Again, it will be like a man going on a journey, who called His servants and entrusted His property to them. (Matthew 25:14)

God owns it all and He has entrusted us with his property. We are stewards, looking after His resources while we are here. He has given us specific gifts and abilities to manage those resources. So what are the consequences?

First, we own nothing. We are stewards. With ownership come rights, with stewardship comes responsibilities. If we are stewards of God's resources, then every spending decision becomes a spiritual decision. Why, because we are being judged by God as we manage His resources.

2. We Are in a Growth Process

His master replied, "Well done good and faithful servant! You have been faithful with a few things; I will put you in charge of many things. Come and share your master's happiness." (Matthew 25:21)

This verse shows that we are to be learning while here on earth, and that we will have rewards in heaven. We are being given money and resources as a tool to be tested and tried. Can we measure up? If we are given tools to learn with, we must be asking "What is it You want me to learn?" If we are to be a good and faithful steward, we must seek Gods guidance to know what is the right thing to do.

Failure to be a good steward has its consequences, as illustrated in the following verse:

And if you have not been trustworthy with someone else's property, who will give you property of your own? (Luke 16:12)

This verse is not about salvation. As believers we are saved. Salvation is by grace not works. However, there are many references in the Bible that are clear about how our rewards in heaven are a function of how we perform here on earth as stewards. We have an eternal life because we are saved. But think about it further. If we perform badly as stewards during our temporary time here we will penalize ourselves in some fashion for eternity. Conversely, if we have done well as stewards for the short time we are here, we have created eternal rewards for ourselves. That should be quite an incentive for a Christian to aspire to be a good steward.

3. The Amount is Not Important

In the parable of the talents, the master rewarded each servant who managed the money, regardless of how well they did. He rewarded them because they tried and were successful to some degree. The point is, it does not matter how much we have to manage, it just matters that we manage it well.

4. Being a Faithful Steward Requires Action

The only servant not rewarded, was the one who hid the money in the ground for fear of losing some if he tried to increase it. He lost everything.

Take the talent from him and give it to the one who has the ten talents. For everyone who has will be given more, and he will have an abundance. Whoever does not have, even what he has will be taken from him. And throw that worthless servant outside, into the darkness, where there will be weeping and gnashing of teeth. (Luke 24:28-30)

Clearly, the servant was punished for being a poor steward. The wicked steward knew what was expected of him, but he failed to act. To be a good steward requires action. Faith without action is insufficient. Any positive action to manage resources will be rewarded. The key here is to have a plan and to act positively.

* * * * *

Letting fear and lack of planning determine your success is a road to failure. Having no plan is tantamount to planning to fail. Any plan is better than no plan. Fear has no place in preparing a financial plan. Fear holds us back and causes us to make poor decisions. We must replace fear with faith. Our faith, combined with our willingness to act will result in blessings. In our hearts we know what we must do but we are often knocked off course by events and reactions to emotion.

The weeping and gnashing of teeth referred to in the verse is something most people can identify with. We are stressed about finances and that negatively impacts our lives. Our lack of faith and planning deprives us of the fruits of the spiritual life and being a good steward. It deprives us of joy, peace and even the material things we desire. If we are diligent we will have all we need. If we want the fruits we must have a plan, even if it is imperfect, and subject to change. With God's guidance we will succeed.

So what does it take to be a good steward? Since we are managing God's resources for him, it must be to attain His goals. If we succeed, we will achieve our goals as well. As Ron Blue puts it, stewardship is the use of God-given resources for God-given goals.

Every Spending Decision Has a Lifetime Impact

A key principle is that money can only be spent once, and on mutually exclusive things. Therefore, how we spend our money today will impact our lives in the future in some degree. At the most basic level, we can choose to spend or save.

For example, let us look at how we might spend $100. We could do one of the following:

- Buy an expensive meal
- Buy an expensive shirt
- Pay off a debt (credit card balance) that has 18% interest accruing
- Invest it at 10% a year and leave it there for 10 or 20 years.

In the first case we will certainly have a nice experience. The meal may even be memorable for a while, but we will soon be hungry and need to eat again.

In the second case we will have a shirt that may last for many years and make us feel good when we wear it, but it may go out of style, or it could be lost or damaged.

Paying off the credit card debt will save $18 over a year that we could use for something else. If we leave the debt for five years, making no payments, we will owe $2228.78. Paying off a debt will save significant money in the future and free up funds for other uses.

Lastly, investing the $100 for 10 or 20 years at 10% will yield a sum of $259.37 or $672.75.

Clearly how we choose to spend that $100 will have current and future impacts on our lives. Not only is that true for our earthly lives, it is even more true for our eternal lives. If we make good spending (stewardship) decisions we benefit now and for eternity. Unfortunately, the converse is also true. Poor spending (stewardship) decisions negatively impacts our earthly and eternal lives.

So, if every spending decision has a life-time and eternal impact, does that not suggest we should take some time to ask ourselves how we should spend and manage the money God entrusts to us? The benefit of a plan is that one can sit down and reflect on the important goals and objectives, decide on priorities and make specific commitment decisions that will work to achieve the goals we have set. Failure to do that will in all likelihood lead to spending decisions that are counter-productive to what we want to achieve, giving us the type of stress we really want to avoid, and depriving ourselves of the things that really matter most to us. More importantly, we will fall short of the test we were given as stewards, with all the consequences that flow from that.

In the sections that follow, we will look at some principles and techniques th will be helpful in being good stewards.

The Household Budget

The most fundamental aspect of a financial plan is the household budget. The va majority of households do not have a budget that allocates spending and savin to achieve family objectives. The household budget reflects the revenues of th household and the priority of spending decisions needed to provide for th household's current and future needs. This is a fundamental responsibility for Christian.

If anyone does not provide for his relatives, and especially for his immediate family, he h denied the faith and is worse than an unbeliever. (1 Timothy 5:8)

The lack of a plan is often at the root of failure in managing our resources. A a consequence, most people are living beyond their means, stressed about th amount of debt they have, and fearful for their future because they do not believ they will have enough when they retire. There is a sense of failure and lack of jo in life. Despite all the spending decisions made, there is paradoxically no true jo and peace.

Budgets are essential for good stewardship. Governments, companies an institutions all operate with them. Having a budget does not guarantee succes but it will mitigate negative consequences. A good budget will achieve its primar objectives. Any budget or plan will have to change over time, because not a future events can be known. Nevertheless, despite short-term adjustments, th overall strategy and objectives can remain intact. The tactics to achieve thos objectives may have to be altered given new circumstances. The key is that th end is always in sight and the focus is not lost. That will provide for the greates degree of success, especially if those goals are consistent with God's plan for ou lives.

The Budget

The household budget is a way to manage the cash flow of the household. Th two main components are revenues and spending.

Revenues will include all sources of income:

- Wages and salaries
- Investment income
- Other income

Expenses will include all spending:

- · Food
- · Housing costs (rent or mortgage)
- · Transportation costs
- · Utilities
- · Debt payments
- · Entertainment
- · Clothing
- · Gifts (tithes)
- · Other expenses

If expenses exceed revenues, then either debt is increased or accumulated savings are reduced to finance expenses.

In order to save for the future, there must be a positive margin: expenses must be less than revenue. This margin can then be saved and/or invested to provide for future needs.

Typically, a household has a pretty good idea of the future cash flows (revenues). The big unknowns are expenditures. By deciding in advance on spending priorities, knowing the cash flow you have to work with, it is possible to plan for savings.

The biggest stewardship challenges facing most households are

1. Containing expenses to the revenue flows so as to have a breakeven or positive margin
2. Managing debt payments and reducing debt
3. Choosing a mortgage and paying it off
4. Saving for a child's education
5. Saving for retirement

We won't get into the area of budgeting, but we will review a few key areas that prove to be challenging for most households. But before we do that it is important to recognize one very important financial reality and that is the magic of compound interest.

The Magic of Compound Interest

When one borrows one pays interest to the lender. When one invests or saves one receives interest or a return. The magic of compounding is that interest can earn interest. The financial implications of this are enormous.

The table below shows what $1 will be worth at various times in the future if it is invested at various rates of return and the interest earned on the dollar stays reinvested through the time period.

Investment Period	The Future Value of $1 Invested at Various Rates of Return								
	Investment Rate of Return								
	3%	5%	8%	10%	12%	15%	18%	20%	25%
3 Years	1.093	1.158	1.260	1.331	1.405	1.521	1.643	1.728	1.953
5 Years	1.159	1.276	1.469	1.611	1.762	2.011	2.288	2.488	3.052
10 Years	1.344	1.629	2.159	2.594	3.106	4.046	5.234	6.192	9.313
15 Years	1.558	2.079	3.172	4.177	5.474	8.137	11.974	15.407	28.422
20 Years	1.806	2.653	4.661	6.727	9.646	16.367	27.393	38.338	86.736
25 Years	2.094	3.386	6.848	10.835	17.000	32.919	62.669	95.396	264.698
30 Years	2.427	4.322	10.063	17.449	29.960	66.212	143.371	237.376	807.794

This table is important in evaluating spending vs investment decisions. The reason is that $1 spent today means foregoing that dollar and earned interest in the future. In economics this is called the opportunity cost. Let's look at an example. Suppose we have $1,000 and we could either spend it on, say a couch, or invest it at 10% for 10 years. The couch does not cost just $1,000. It really costs $2,594 (2.594 in the 10% column on the 10-year row, times $1,000) because that is what we would have earned if we had invested that money instead.

If all spending decisions are looked at in this context we really understand that spending decisions have lifetime implications.

The flip side of this table is the cost of debt. If we borrow $1000 at 10% to buy the couch the total outlay to buy the couch is $2,594. But the true cost is even higher when we add in the opportunity cost. Let us assume for simplicity that we pay $259.40 each year in ten equal payments. If that money was invested at 10% a year, the total after ten years is $4,547. The true cost of a $1,000 couch financed at 10% over 10 years is actually $4,547, because that is the income forgone to buy the couch.

The Role of Debt

The rich rule over the poor, and the borrower is the servant to the lender. (Proverbs 22:7)

In today's society it is so easy to get credit to finance our whims and desires. Consequently, debt is a major problem for most people. Debt is insidious and enslaves us just as the Scriptures say. Once we take on debt we are working for the lender. We become a slave to them. We have lost flexibility and freedom. We now have a contractual commitment to spend some of our future income in a manner we cannot easily alter. Unfortunately, we continue to pay well after the benefits of the financed purchase have all but disappeared.

Credit card debt is the worst kind of debt, since it carries interest costs of up to 30% or more. Credit card companies make it easy to pay small amounts to stay current and will even extend more credit if payments are consistently paid. People on the debt treadmill find that they often have to take out more debt to make debt payments. Unless checked, this will ultimately lead to financial ruin.

Mortgage debt is another common form of debt. It is usually necessary in order to purchase a home. Because compounding has such significance it is important to really understand the different costs associated with mortgages. The interest paid, the amortization period, the number of payments made and the periodic additional payments will all have a significant impact on the final cost of a mortgage.

Term debt is typically used for purchasing durables such as cars, furniture, etc.

Getting into debt is very easy, getting out of debt is very difficult. Many people who do not have a budget or financial plan to get out of debt stay caught in a debt spiral and suffer for it.

It is ironic that people who do not want the perceived limiting effects of a budget or financial plan will actually take on debt. Debt is much more limiting to your choices than a plan or budget. A plan to avoid debt or get out of debt provides freedom in the future.

When Should Debt be Used?

There are appropriate times to use debt. However, it is very important to know the full costs of debt in order to manage your expenses and be a good steward.

Debt should be used as a last resort and only for something that is really needed, not just desired. It is best if the after-tax cost of the debt is less than the yield that will be earned on the item bought with the debt.

Credit Card Debt

Some would argue that credit card debt should never be used. However, in today's world a credit card is essential. It is virtually impossible to purchase electronically or rent a car or check into a hotel unless you have a credit card.

The key to credit card debt is to never let the monthly balance be carried over. Using the credit card as an effective interest-free loan when the balance is paid off before the grace period ends is a way to keep your own funds earning a return.

Mortgage Debt

Mortgage debt is a huge financial commitment. It pays to shop around for the best rate and also the best payment terms. Even small differences can amount to savings of tens of thousands of dollars and speed up the payment of the mortgage to make you mortgage free.

The table below shows the differences in payments, total interest paid, and the effective amortization period for mortgages, using different payment methods and interest rates.

Mortgage Options and Costs for $100,000

Mortgage Rate	Payment Schedule		Total Interest Paid		Years to Pay Off	
	Bi-weekly	Monthly	Bi-weekly	Monthly	Bi-weekly	Monthly
Amortization Period = 25 Years						
6.00	319.91	639.81	74,335	91,941	21.0	25.0
6.25	327.37	654.74	77,368	96,423	20.8	25.0
6.50	334.91	669.82	80,367	100,949	20.7	25.0
6.75	342.53	685.05	83,325	105,515	20.6	25.0
7.00	356.10	700.42	86,252	110,123	20.5	25.0
Amortization Period = 20 Years						
6.00	356.10	712.19	59,272	70,925	17.2	20.0
6.25	363.14	726.28	61,772	74,308	17.1	20.0
6.50	370.25	740.50	64,072	77,720	17.0	20.0
6.75	377.42	754.84	66,733	81,164	17.0	20.0
7.00	384.66	769.31	68,979	84,635	16.9	20.0
Amortization Period = 15 Years						
6.00	419.94	839.88	43,993	51,179	13.2	15.0
6.25	426.54	853.08	45,876	53,553	13.2	15.0
6.50	433.19	866.37	47,757	55,946	13.1	15.0
6.75	439.88	879.76	49,638	58,357	13.1	15.0
7.00	446.63	893.25	51,515	60,785	13.0	15.0

Source: www.royalbank.com

Mortgage Rate

Even small savings on the mortgage rate can save thousands of dollars in interest over the life of the mortgage. For example, as the next chart shows, the total interest paid on a $100,000 mortgage with monthly payments

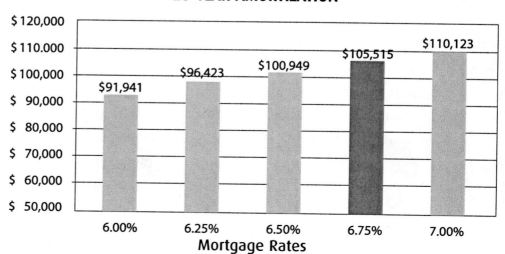

TOTAL INTEREST PAID ON $100,00 MORTGAGE
25-YEAR AMORTIZATION

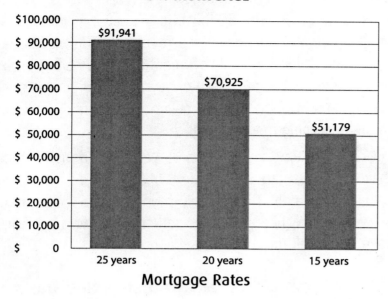

**TOTAL INTEREST PAID ON $100,00
6% MORTGAGE**

$91,941

$70,925

$51,179

25 years   20 years   15 years

Mortgage Rates

amortized over 25 years at 6% instead of 6.25% will be $91.941 instead of $96,423, a savings of $4,482. The monthly payment drops from $654.74 to $639.81, a saving of $14.93 a month.

Saving 4% (.25% of 6.25%) on the mortgage rate saves 2.2% on the mortgage payment but eventually 4.6% on the total amount of interest paid.

Banks and credit unions are very competitive and may negotiate rates down from their posted levels. It will pay off to deal with several institutions to negotiate the lowest rate possible. A saving of half a percent could amount to over $9,000.

Amortization Period

The amortization period is the length of time it takes to pay off the mortgage. The shorter the amortization period, the less the total interest paid and the sooner you will be mortgage-free.

For example, assume you get a 6% mortgage on $100,000. If the amortization period is 25 years, the total interest paid is $91,941 compared to $70,925 for a 20-year amortization period and $51,179 for a 15-year period. Shortening the amortization period will set you mortgage-free earlier and free up cash flow for other uses, such as charitable donations, vacations, children's education, a new car or retirement savings.

The negative aspect of shortening the amortization period is it will increase the monthly payments. This may create a cash flow burden. However, if the higher monthly payments can be afforded, then the total cost savings are very large.

Payment Frequency

Choosing your mortgage payment frequency can also have a major impact on total interest savings as well as the effective time it takes to pay off a mortgage. For example, a bi-weekly payment will result in 26 payments a year compared to 12 for a monthly payment. Because part of each payment is principal, the greater the frequency of payments the greater the reduction in principal, upon which the interest owing is calculated. Interest owing is calculated on a declining monthly balance.

On a 6% $100,000 mortgage with a 25-year amortization period the total interest paid declines from $91,941 to $74,335 just by paying every two weeks instead of monthly. The monthly payments are the same except for two months in which there are three rather than two payments. The bi-weekly payment is half the monthly payment.

INTEREST PAID VS AMORTIZATION PERIOD AND PAYMENT FREQUENCY

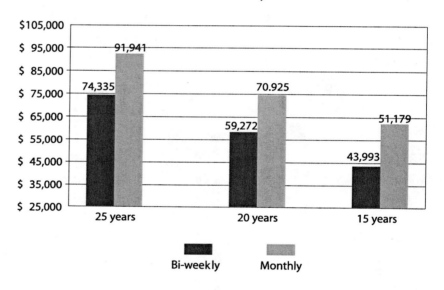

The bi-weekly payment also effectively reduces your amortization period. For example, on a 25-year mortgage the amortization drops to 21 years at 6% interest. This pays the mortgage off 4 years ahead of schedule. Similarly the bi-weekly payment reduces a 20-year amortization to 17.2 years and a 15-year amortization period to 13.2 years, all at a 6% mortgage rate.

Thus, depending on the household's financial circumstances and ability to afford higher monthly payments, there are great savings on housing if the amortization can be shortened and the payments made bi-weekly. In our example of a $100,000 mortgage at 6% the worst case scenario is a monthly payment of $639.81 on a 25-year amortization. The total interest paid is $91,941 and the mortgage is paid off in 25 years. BY increasing the payments to a monthly equivalent of $839.88, and paying bi-weekly on a 15-year amortization, the total interest paid is $43,993, and the mortgage is paid off in 13.2 years.

Savings and Investing

Many people find it hard to save, rationalizing that saving small amounts won't make any difference to their future. This attitude prevents people from securing their financial future, reducing financial stress and giving them the financial freedom God has in store for each of us.

The belief that small amounts do not matter is false and leads to many wrong spending decisions. If we apply the magic of compounding to even small amounts of savings over long time periods, it can add up to substantial dollars.

It is not uncommon for people to spend $10 per week on the lottery in the hopes that one day they will win big, even if not the jackpot. Surveys of Canadians show that buying lottery tickets on a regular basis is part of the retirement savings strategy for about 30% of the population. At the root of this is the lack of understanding of the magic of compound interest and the rewards of a disciplined approach.

The table below shows the value of saving $10 per week or $50 bi-weekly over an extended period under several different annual rates of return. The results are quite impressive.

Putting $10 a week into the bank at an average rate of 3% will amount to just under $10,000 in 15 years, and just over $32,000 in 35 years.

· If one gets a little more aggressive with the investment and buys a conservative bond mutual fund with a 5% annual return then the amounts increase to almost $12,000 in 15 years and just over $49,000 in 35 years.

· If the investments were in a balanced mutual fund the returns are even greater, with over $18,000 in 15 years and over $155,000 in 35 years.

· If the money was invested in something that averaged 15% a year the total would exceed $1 million in 35 years.

The table underscores one very important feature of investing start early, even with small amounts.

Take a 30-year old couple today. If they start saving $10 a week and earn 5% a year they will have $36,275 by the time they reach 60. If they wait until they are 40 to start saving at that rate they have only $18,054 at age 60. That is a loss of $18,221 by not investing $1,040 in their thirties. If they wait until they are 50 to start saving the losses are even greater. They will have accumulated only $6,867. This illustrates the magic of compounding. For the magic of compounding to really work it is important to give it as much time as possible.

It is not impossible to become a millionaire if you are a good steward, start a regular savings plan and stick to it. Look at how the 15% return creates $1.22 million by investing just $50 bi-weekly for 35 years. A total of $45,500 was saved, so the difference of $1.17 million was all interest earned on interest. Another illustration of the magic of compound interest.

How Does One Go About Investing?

There are many different ways to invest. There are term deposits available at banks, trust companies and credit unions. One can buy stocks and bonds. One can buy mutual funds which all carry varying degrees of risk. The returns one can expect reflect the short-term risks and volatility in the investment vehicle chosen. For example, term deposits at a major financial institution carry virtually no risk and are guaranteed by the government to a fixed amount. Commensurately, the returns are low in the 3% to 5% range mostly, although there was a period of much higher rates when inflation was high. The highest degree of risk, at least in the categories we are discussing, are in stocks and some corporate bonds.

Just as the servants in the parable of the talents are charged by the master to look after his money, we as stewards of God's resources are charged with growing his money. And recall what happened to the lazy steward who hid the money in the ground? His was a riskless strategy akin to us putting God's resources in term deposits. His reward was that he lost all that he had. God took it away from him.

The three most important biblical principles of investing are:

1. Trust in the Lord, seek His guidance in devising an investment plan.

Commit to the Lord whatever you do, and your plans will succeed (Proverbs 16:3)

2. Diversify investments to reduce risk

Give portions to seven, yes to eight, for you do not know what disaster may come upon the land (Ecclesiastes 11:2)

3. Avoid get-rich-quick schemes

The plans of the diligent lead to profit as surely as haste leads to poverty (Proverbs 21:5)

4. Know when to buy and sell to reduce risk and improve returns

The prudent man sees danger and takes refuge, but the simple keep going and suffer for it. (Proverbs 22:3)

HOW TO GET OUT OF DEBT

Step 1

- Stop buying on your credit card and commit to putting all extra income into debt retirement.

Step 2

- Prioritize spending
- Start giving a percentage to God's storehouse.
- Start a savings plan with a goal of saving 10 % of income
- Then allocate the remainder to spending plan items.

Step 3

- Sell all depreciating items for which you are now in debt.
- Replace with less expensive items.
- Get out from under all unnecessary monthly payments.
- Sell all items with maintenance and upkeep costs first.
- Sell all items paid for but not being used.

Step 4

- Closely examine food costs. You should be able to make a 15% cut.

Step 5

- Begin immediately to learn to do it yourself, instead of paying for services.

Step 6

- Write to all the people you owe—DO NOT CALL THEM!
- Acknowledge your debts
- Tell them how you intend to pay
- Tell them the amount you have allocated to pay them. Then follow through and pay them.
- Ask in the letter if they will consider dropping all financial charges.

Step 7

- Make getting out of debt a prayerful family effort. Let every member participate with his or her own resources.

Step 8

- Plan your own debt elimination.
- Pay the smallest debt off first.
- Double pay on the next smallest debt, etc.

Believe it or Not

- If you buy a regular cup of coffee rather than a latte or espresso and take a brown bag lunch from ages 19-61 you will have accumulated $282,000.00

- Want a Rolex? To purchase a $4,000 Rolex at age 25 you are losing the opportunity to have $68,983 at age 61.

- How much does it cost for one large pizza a week? If you said $250,000, you obviously know a thing or two about investing. Financial planner, Allyson Lewis, author of *The Million Dollar Car and $250,000 Pizza* (Dearborn Trade, 2000), says that if $20 spent on pizza were invested weekly in a mutual fund with a 9% annual return, it would be worth a quarter of a million dollars in 30 years. She calls eating out a "money magnet"—an over-looked expense, like late fees and full-service gas. Here, what these seemingly small expenses would be worth after 20 years in earning a 9% annual interest. —Ken Budd

ITEM	COST	ANNUAL COST	IF YOU INVESTED YOUR MONEY IN 2020 IT WOULD BE
ATM Fees	2.50 per week (Didn't use your own bank)	$130	$7,280
Soda	$.75 per can, 5 Times per week	195	10,192
Pedicure	$35 per session, 4 times per year	210	11,595
Lottery Ticket	$1 per ticket, 5 Times per week	260	13,302
Frozen Yogurt	$3 for a large (with sprinkles) 2 times per week	312	15,962
Cigars	$5 per stogie (box of 25), 4 boxes per year	500	25,580
Mocha Latté	$3 per grande, 5 Times per week	780	43,682
Movie Tickets	$20 per week (2 tickets, popcorn, soda)	1,040	53,207
Women's Shoes	$70 per pair, 15 per year	1,050	53,718
Dinner for Two (out)	$50 per dinner, 2 times per week	5,200	291,214

Saving is like shaving.
If you don't do a little of it
each day, you're a bum.

Please let us know!

How has God touched your life after studying His principles for spiritual and financial success? Please tick the appropriate response and mail this page to us. Not only will it give us an opportunity to pray for you, but if we include‹ your story in our next book, your example may also be a blessing to others.

❑ Have you invited Jesus Christ to be your personal Saviour and Lord as a result of studying *Seeds of Success?*

❑ Have you rededicated your life to God while studying this book?

❑ Have you experienced financial blessing as you started to pay your tithes?

❑ Have you experienced miraculous increase in your finances as you started to apply God's principles of planting and harvesting?

❑ Have you experienced healing as you obeyed and brought your tithes and offerings to God?

❑ Would you like to receive more information about Total Success Ministries?

Please send your response to

Total Success Ministries

11071-160A St.

Surrey, BC

V4N 4R5

Canada

You may also e-mail us at:

indirapatro@shaw.ca

Or visit our website at

www.totalsuccess.org

ISBN 155369215-2

9 781553 692157